Understanding God's Great Plan

A JEWISH, CHRISTIAN, BIBLE PERSPECTIVE

Dr. Peter Wyns

Copyright Reserved

Understanding God's Great Plan
$14.95

Copyright ©2020 by Dr. Peter Wyns

To contact the author, please write to the below postal or email address:

Christians For Messiah Ministries
PO Box 36324
Rock Hill, SC 29732
Email: wynsusa@comporium.net

All scriptures taken from the New International Version unless otherwise noted.

Scriptures taken from the Holy Bible, New International Version ©

All rights reserved. No part of this publication may be reproduced without prior permission of Christians for Messiah Publishing or Dr. Peter Wyns

First Great Reward Publishing edition published 2020

Cover Design by: Judy Wilson

Editing by: Jesse Enns, Elizabeth Enns, Strachelle Wyns, Joy Wyns

Manufactured in the United States of America by Ingram Spark

ISBN: 978-0-9915421-9-2

DEDICATION

I am glad to dedicate this book to the five-fold ministers that God has sent into the world. They are pastors, evangelists, prophets, teachers and apostles.

While privileged beyond measure, to serve the Lord as special ambassadors, they carry an enormous weight of almost unbearable responsibility.

They struggle to be unified in vision and in care one for another. None of them sees all that is in the heart of God and yet they must press forward to lead the saints and bring them into the great plans of God.

They are amazing people and I am eternally grateful for their sacrifice and resolve. They bear the marks of serving the Lord in their bodies and in their souls. Their golden rewards are eternal.

I am humbled to be counted as one, almost insignificant member, of that great company. Help me Lord to do my part.

Peter Wyns

Introduction

UNDERSTANDING GOD'S GREAT PLAN is an overview of what God planned before He made the world. Although many lengthy books could be written on the subject, this book was intentionally kept brief so it would be an easy read for everyone. At present, all of us are in the middle of God's great plan. Once understood, His plan will transform our attitudes and behavior and lead us to a broader, kingdom-of-God, perspective.

I understand that there are many different perspectives on eschatology and good Bible teachers may not agree with all that I have written in this book. Each Bible teacher is responsible to teach the revelation that they have. This is what I believe God has revealed in the Bible. I trust you will find it helpful.

From a great family of Bible teachers, and more than fifty years of ministry, I give what insight I have gained on this topic. My source is the Bible, and even though I think God's great plan is clearly revealed in scripture, I believe it has been overlooked by many.

Other books have been written on God's ultimate intention and all the ones I have read have been instructive. From what I have seen, however, many essential dynamics are missing in those books.

Understanding God's Great Plan presents aspects of Messianic, Jewish, and Christian perspectives of purpose and faith, and combines them in one teaching.

This book is a valuable tool for any Bible student because it answers the major questions of life and faith as revealed in scripture. Here are some of those questions.

Why did God create the universe?
Why did God create the world?
Why did God make the nations?
Why is Jerusalem important?
Why are the Jews important?
Why did God give us the Law of Moses?
Why did God give us the ark of the covenant?
Why did He give us Jesus?
Why must Jesus have preeminence?
Why did God give us the Holy Spirit?
Why did God make the human race?
Why did God invent marriage?
Why do people sin?
Why is there a devil?
Why did Jesus come to die?

Introduction

Why are people called to the ministry?
Why does God have a church?
Why is church government important?
Why did God create discipleship?
What is the family of God?
Where will the government center of the universe be in the future?
What is God's ultimate intention for humanity?
Is there life on other planets?
What will we do in eternity?

These and other Bible questions are answered in brief in this book. You may be surprised at some of the answers.

The Lord told Daniel that in the last days, new revelation will be released that previously had been hidden from view. In the end, the wise will see and understand more of God's master plan, but the wicked will not understand.

"Daniel, roll up and seal the words of the scroll until the time of the end"..."How long will it be before these astonishing things are fulfilled?"... "Go your way Daniel, because the words are rolled up and sealed until the time of the end. Many will be purified, made spotless and refined, but the wicked will continue to be wicked. None of the wicked will understand, but those who are wise will understand." Dan. 12:4,6,9,10

We are now in that time period of new revelation

that Daniel spoke of; therefore, we can expect fresh insight. When new truth comes, let it be tested and let it line up with scripture. In light of these verses in Daniel, we should prepare ourselves for new revelation and a shift in our traditional thinking.

Table of Contents

PART ONE
Thrones

Chapter One
God and His Son 3

Chapter Two
The Thrones of God and The Lamb 11

Chapter Three
God Making Plans 21

Chapter Four
The Foundation Stone. 33

Chapter Five
The Ark of the Covenant 45

PART TWO
Who is Man that You are Mindful of Him?

Chapter Six
The Journey of Man 59

Chapter Seven
Why the Church? 69

Chapter Eight
God's Government 77

Chapter Nine
The Harvest 85

Chapter Ten
Called into Fellowship........................97

PART THREE
A Kingdom Without End

Chapter Eleven
Myriads of Angels 107

Chapter Twelve
The Second Coming 115

Chapter Thirteen
The Millennial Kingdom..................... 123

Chapter Fourteen
Life in the Millennium 133

Chapter Fifteen
New Physics................................ 141

Chapter Sixteen
World Without End 151

PART ONE

Thrones

CHAPTER ONE

God and His Son

The Beginning

Call it the big bang, creation, or just the beginning, but the universe started at a singular point and God was there. His Son, Jesus, is called "The Word," and all things were made through Him.

"In the beginning was the Word, and the Word was with God, and the Word was God. He was with God in the beginning. Through him all things were made; without him nothing was made that has been made." Jn. 1:1-3

Unequivocally, God's eternal plan focuses on His Son, "The Word." Everything was made by Him and for Him (see Rev. 4:1 KJV).

For many Bible students, this first chapter may seem obvious; nevertheless, Jesus is the focus of this chapter. Starting with Jesus as the central theme cannot be circumnavigated; Jesus is God's eternal plan.

The Christian faith has taught us about Jesus, but many other details of God's plan have not been taught. I trust that this book will bring fresh revelation to help increase your understanding. My aim is to give you a larger overview, but the most essential theme of God's plan will always be Jesus the Messiah, Yeshua Hamashiach. That is how you say Jesus Christ in Hebrew. (Jesus is actually the Greek word for Joshua. The "J" is pronounced "Y" in Hebrew, which gives us Yeshua).

Kids say Amazing Things

I have discovered that my children and grandchildren are brilliant. Starting at a young age they loved to grapple with the eternal questions of life. When my daughter Rachel, who is now in her 40s, was just five, she said, "Dad, I don't get it. How can God exist before the beginning? I just don't get it."

I told her, "I don't know Rachel. All I know is that Jesus was there when everything began and He made it all."

That is what the Bible teaches, so I believe it. From beginning to end, God's master plan is about Jesus.

"The Son is the image of the invisible God, the firstborn over all creation. For in him all things were created: things in heaven and on earth, visible

and invisible, whether thrones or powers or rulers or authorities; all things have been created through him and for him. He is before all things and in him all things hold together. And he is the head of the body, the church, he is the beginning and the firstborn from among the dead, so that in everything he might have the supremacy." Col. 1:15-18

The words are finite; Jesus is God, He created all things, He has all power, He was before all things, and everything continues to hold together because of Him.

Even More Remarkable

Personally, for me, there is something even more remarkable than God's greatness. It is the fact that God chose to bring us into this equation. From the beginning, He chose to make people part of His family. He calls us His body, the Church, the called out ones.

This is how He did it. Jesus left the infinite realm of heaven and came to us in a finite world. He became a flesh-and-blood man in order to bring us into His divine family. To do this, He had to make us holy, as He is holy, so Jesus died to pay for our unholiness. Then, because our sin was removed, He was able to adopt us into His family. He gave us the power to become His sons and daughters. He justifies, sanctifies and glorifies us. That means, as His kids, we will inherit all things along with Jesus.

"He who did not spare his own Son, but gave him up for us all—how will he not also, along with him, graciously give us all things." Rom. 8:32

His plan led Christ to His death but also to His resurrection. He was the first to be raised from the dead (to a non-dying life) and His plan opened the door for us to follow in the resurrection. Jesus is the beginning and the end and He will bring us through a resurrection and establish us as permanent family members for all eternity.

Apostolic Resolve

The early apostles made Jesus' death and resurrection the main focus of their teaching. Paul said, *"I resolved to know nothing while I was with you except Jesus Christ and him crucified." 1 Cor. 2:2*

Peter said, *"He has given us new birth into a living hope through the resurrection of Jesus Christ from the dead." 1 Pet. 1:3*

Peter also said, *"Salvation is found in no one else, for there is no other name under heaven given to mankind by which we must be saved." Acts 4:12*

God's eternal plan is magnificent. If, however, we could not be part of it, it would be the ultimate letdown. The apostles realized that Jesus, God's Son, was and is the way for us to become God's family.

Paul said, *"For God was pleased to have all his*

fullness dwell in him [In Christ], *and through him to reconcile to himself all things, whether things on earth or things in heaven, by making peace through his blood, shed on the cross." Col. 1:19-20*

Jesus paid for man's sin and reconciled the world to Himself. He is the ruler of everything and He is the only one who can hold it all together. The human race is sinful and messy and would be unfixable without His rule.

Hell in a House

As a pastor, I have visited families where domestic violence was erupting. Husbands and wives were at each other's throats, teens were in rebellion, and life was spiraling out of control. Family dysfunction causes pain. It brings anger, bitterness, alienation, divorce, poverty, sickness and even murder.

My task in going to such a home was to help bring peace. Sometimes, I was successful and sometimes things were irreconcilable. In the worst situations, the police were brought in. In the best situations, family members called upon the Lord Jesus, and through repentance, forgiveness, and love, healing came and peace was restored.

The Bible says, *"Every house* [family] *is built by someone... Christ is faithful as the Son over God's house* [family]. *And we are his house* [family].*" Heb. 3:4,6*

Most homes, even those without Christ, are not

filled with violence, but without Jesus, the human race will end up in violence. In the time of Noah the world was destroyed because of violence. Since then, violence has accelerated throughout history, and it seems there is no end of it in sight.

Jesus is God and is worthy of the highest place. As the Creator, He earned the right to rule over all that He has made. Then, He became a man and died for the entire human race and earned the right to be supreme ruler once again (see Phil. 2:8-11). He is also the only one who can maintain peace and harmony. That is another reason why Jesus must be head over all things.

Exalted to the Highest Place

The Church is God's family but Jesus' government extends further than the human race. During His thousand-year reign on earth, the Lord will make the whole planet right.

We read, *"The Lord will be king over the whole earth. On that day there will be one Lord, and his name the only name." Zech. 14:9*

Jesus has preeminence over all that He has made; He is supreme.

"He humbled himself by becoming obedient to death - even death on a cross! Therefore God exalted him [Jesus] *to the highest place and gave him a name*

that is above every name, that at the name of Jesus every knee should bow, in heaven and on earth and under the earth, and every tongue acknowledge that Jesus Christ is Lord, to the glory of God the Father." Phil. 2:8-11

We conclude this chapter by saying that the first detail of God's master plan is that Jesus Christ is King of kings and Lord of lords, and that in all things, He alone has the first place, and it will always be that way.

CHAPTER TWO

The Throne of God and The Lamb

Ruling From Jerusalem

After His second coming, Jesus' throne will be in Jerusalem. Here is a glimpse of Jesus governing from His throne on the Temple Mount.

"In the last days the mountain of the Lord's temple will be established as chief among the mountains; it will be raised above the hills, and all nations will stream to it. Many peoples will come and say, "Come, let us go up to the mountain of the Lord, to the house of the God of Jacob. He will teach us his ways, so that we may walk in his paths." The law will go out from Zion, the word of the Lord from Jerusalem. He will judge between the nations and will settle disputes for

many peoples. They will beat their swords into plowshares and their spears into pruning hooks. Nation will not take up sword against nation, nor will they train for war anymore. Come, O house of Jacob, let us walk in the light of the Lord." Isa. 2:2-5

Scripture says that in the last days, people and nations will stream to Jerusalem. Jesus will sit enthroned as a judge, settling disputes. He will teach the nations how to coexist in righteousness and peace. The world will live in harmony and be blessed. His rule will emanate from the Temple Mount in Jerusalem (in this scripture it is called, the mountain of the Lord's temple).

While Jerusalem does have a spiritual counterpart called the New Jerusalem, the above verse speaks clearly of a physical Jerusalem in Israel. This is an important detail. Some would have us believe that God's Jerusalem is only a spiritual entity and the physical one in the Middle East has no spiritual significance. I believe that nothing could be further from the truth. The physical Jerusalem, as described in the aforementioned scripture, gives us a proper perspective of the importance of the present day Israel, and the physical Temple Mount, that we see in Jerusalem.

Affection for Jerusalem

The physical Jerusalem in Israel cannot be overlooked. It is of immense importance and the Lord has great affection for it. Have you ever wondered why the Bible places such an enormous emphasis on the Jews, Israel, and Jerusalem?

The focus on them is absolutely overwhelming in the Scriptures. After the first eleven chapters of the Bible, the Old Testament is all about the Jews, their spiritual history, and their walk with God. The New Testament is about Jesus and His ministry to the Jewish people, and about the Jewish apostles and their ministry that starts in Israel and goes to the nations.

We may ask ourselves, "Why is Jerusalem so important?" For me the answer is clear. Remembering Jerusalem with great affection is an essential matter with God because it represents the future rule and government of Jesus on earth. It depicts His reign, His care for people, and His love for the planet. Ultimately, He will not allow us to ignore His plans for the physical city of Jerusalem. Look at what scripture says about it.

"If I forget you, O Jerusalem, may my right hand forget its skill. May my tongue cling to the roof of my mouth, if I do not remember you" Ps. 137:5-6 (Emphasis added)

Some rabbinical scholars attribute the writing of this Psalm to the prophet Jeremiah. In it, he laments over Jerusalem and shares its importance, as he sees it. I believe he carries the heart of God for this chosen place.

Do you understand what this scripture is saying? Your right hand represents the best of everything about you. Without remembering Jerusalem, Jeremiah believes he will not be at his best. He will make wrong choices and his life will lack its best achievements. His right hand will lose its cunning. To Jeremiah, forgetting Jerusalem is the same as forgetting a major part of the government and plans of God.

The late Derek Prince, my grandfather, used to say that Israel was extremely important to God. It is like the first button while buttoning up your shirt. If you get the first button in the wrong hole, then all of the other buttons will end up in the wrong holes. If you don't love Jerusalem, the rest of your theology will be out of whack because Jesus ruling from Jerusalem is central to God's master plan.

If we take the words of Jeremiah as God's words for us, then forgetting Jerusalem will cause you to circumnavigate God's plan, and Jeremiah says that will result in some kind of personal judgment against you. As the above scripture reveals, the first judgment involves your right hand, the second involves your tongue. If you bypass and ignore Jerusalem, your tongue clings to the roof of your mouth. This is a picture of dire thirst and ill health. It speaks of drought in your life and an enormous lack of that which satisfies.

Your Highest Joy

Let's refer to this Bible text about Jerusalem again, and this time let's look at the last part of the verse.

"If I forget you, O Jerusalem, may my right hand forget its skill. May my tongue cling to the roof of my mouth if I do not remember you, if I do not consider Jerusalem my highest joy." Ps. 137:5-6

Even lovers of Israel may struggle with Jeremiah's word when he says that he should make Jerusalem his highest joy. He was a prophet of the Lord and his writings are part of the Holy Scriptures.

Should not Jesus, should not God, be our highest joy? After all, the Bible commands us to follow two rules: Love God with all your heart and love your neighbor as yourself. I believe those are really the two main commandments in the Bible and all others are given to help us understand and do those two things.

In order to love God with all of your heart, however, you must love everything about Him. You cannot love God and reject His commandments, His government, His plans or His ways. If you love Him with all of your heart, you love all the details that He presents to you.

That is what Jerusalem represented to Jeremiah. To me, it represents the details of His future government on earth. I believe that Jerusalem is God's focus when He looks at the earth. Scripture says that His eyes and His heart will always be there (see 2 Chr. 7:16). It represents a focus on the future of His Son's reign. Jesus' throne will be in Jerusalem. It will be His seat of government. It is the place from where He will release His glory and His goodness over people, over the world and over the universe. There are many other verses in the Bible that lead us to this conclusion. As we go forward in this book, we will study some of them.

The Joy of the Whole Earth

In the following verse, the Lord gives Jerusalem a variety of names or accolades; Mount Zion, the city of the Great King, His holy mountain and the joy of the whole earth. We see that Jesus is worthy to be praised as He sits enthroned in the city of God. Mount Zion is beautiful in its loftiness. The entire world will burst forth with unparalleled joy when Jesus takes His place on Mount Zion and rules from Jerusalem.

"Great is the Lord, and most worthy of praise, in the city of our God, his holy mountain. It is beautiful in its loftiness, <u>the joy of the whole earth</u>. Like the utmost heights of Zaphon is Mount Zion, the city of the Great King." Ps. 48:1-2 (Emphasis added)

To further emphasize this passion, the Lord has set watchmen on Zion's walls. They are intercessors from all around the world that have been commissioned to pray until Jerusalem becomes the praise of the whole earth. Read the next verse.

"I have posted watchmen on your walls, O Jerusalem; they will never be silent day or night. You who call on the Lord, give yourselves no rest... and give him no rest till he establishes Jerusalem and makes her the praise of the earth." Isa. 62:6-7

Presently, the Lord is focused on establishing Israel for His end-time purpose and, ultimately, for His throne. He is not passive about this and neither should you be.

The Lord says, *"For Zion's sake I will not keep silent, for <u>Jerusalem's sake</u> I will not remain quiet, till her righteousness shines out like the dawn, her salvation like a blazing torch. The nations will see your righteousness and all kings your glory; you will be called by a new name that the mouth of the Lord will bestow. You will be a crown of splendor in the Lord's hand, a royal diadem in the hand of your God." Isa. 62:1-3* (Emphasis added)

The Throne of God and of the Lamb

To find out more of the endgame of God's master plan, we look at the book of Revelation. In the last chapter of the last book of the Bible, we read, *"The throne of God and of the Lamb will be in that city." Rev. 22:3*

That city is Jerusalem. There are two applications in Scripture regarding the city of Jerusalem: The earthy one, in Israel, and the New Jerusalem, which is made up of all the people of God. The New Jerusalem is called, The Mother Of Us All (see Gal. 4:26 KJV). It is the bride of Christ that comes down to earth from heaven when the Lord returns to earth (see Rev. 21:2). The New Jerusalem comes to earth on resurrection day, when the spirits of God's family who are in heaven come to earth with Christ and receive their glorified bodies (see 1 Thes. 4:16, 1 Cor. 15:52, Rev. 19:11-24). (For further details on Christ's return and the resurrection, see my book <u>Unexpected Fire</u>).

I believe the aforementioned Scripture in Revelation 22:3, that speaks of the city where the thrones of God and of Jesus will be, is speaking of both Jerusalems. First of all, God and Jesus will govern over all the people of God, so the throne, or government, will be in the family of God. Scripture also seems to indicate that the physical throne and the new throne room will be on the temple mount in Israel.

Most believers understand that Jesus will bring His throne to Jerusalem, but many have not yet realized that God the Father will also put His throne in that city as well. That is what the Scripture says:

"The throne of God and of the Lamb will be in that city." Rev. 22:3

Planet earth was made for this purpose. Can you see it? Jerusalem is not just the capital city of Israel; it is destined to be the capital city of the whole world. It will be the capital city of the entire universe because God the Father, and the Son, will put their thrones there. From the temple mount in Jerusalem they will rule, manage, and advance the affairs of the entire universe.

At this present time, there is a physical throne room where God sits on a fiery throne. John describes it in Revelation chapters four and five. To me, it is logical that God will have a physical throne room in the future as well. The kingdom of God is coming to earth in full measure, and I believe His throne will be on the temple mount.

Revelation from the Lord's Prayer

When the disciples asked Jesus to teach them how to pray, He took them right to God's master plan. He taught them what we call the Lord's Prayer.

It says, *"Thy kingdom come, Thy will be done on earth as it is in heaven." Mt. 6:26*

Every prayer that Jesus prayed must be answered because He has, from the beginning, designed the future. His kingdom will come to earth just as it is in heaven. In other words, heaven is moving to the earth.

This is not a new idea, nor is it a default plan, if some earlier plan doesn't work. This was God's plan from the beginning. I am convinced that His new throne room is the reason He made the planet. It is the reason for everything He has done in the world. The throne of His Son, and therefore, the city of Jerusalem is His priority.

In the next chapter we will explore this perspective further.

CHAPTER THREE

God Making Plans

Plans

God does not think like us. Actually, we, who are made in His image, tend to think like Him, and He is a creator and a builder.

Recently, my wife and I built a new home. The idea started as a financial plan for retirement. We have worked hard all of our lives and have often thought about saving for retirement. This is a challenge for ministers who are not part of a large denomination because they have no company retirement plan. In order to be responsible, we came up with a plan.

We tried a few times to invest our life savings and our inheritance money, and we almost lost it. We decided to put our money into a lake property on the condition that we could find a parcel of land at a great price. Finally, after years of searching, we refinanced our home and bought four and a half acres of lake property an hour south of where we live.

We bought the property seven years ago, but there was no home on it. Then, last year, we finally paid off our existing home mortgage and decided to invest again by getting a new mortgage and building a new home down at the lake. A great new adventure began.

The new property is wild, with a thick forest and steep hills that open up to a gorgeous view of the lake. I drew up some plans for a dream home that we could afford to build, given the limitations of our new mortgage. Then we faced an unexpected challenge. The land is remote, rugged, and hilly, and no builder wanted to build our home unless we would pay a small fortune. All the builders' prices were way beyond our budget, and we found ourselves at a financial standstill.

Over time, we adjusted our plans, and finally, the fifth contractor that we interviewed agreed to build our home within our budget.

The house is now built. It is a two story solid home with a walk out basement. It boasts a vaulted ceiling with floor to ceiling windows that face the lake. In order to finance the project within our budget, the basement is completely unfinished. Joy and I have now drawn up plans to finish the basement and we are building it with our own hands, as we are able.

As I write this, I am glad to report that we have already begun building the infrastructure of the basement. The upstairs is finished and we are loving our new house. We are thankful to the Lord that this dream has become a reality.

The Lord's Plans

It is somewhat like that with the Lord; He has plans for His future, His family, and His house. His plans, however, include a kingdom without end, that stretches from eternity to eternity, and He has no budget to contend with. Like us, He has hired laborers. Not out of necessity, but by design, He chose others to build with Him. Those workers are His people.

There is a problem, however. Not all who could be co-builders want to partner with the Lord, and many who say yes to helping Him build, do not want to build it His way. Many have not focused on His master plan, nor have they studied the blueprints sufficiently. So, even though they want to build, they may not have the right vision or perspective.

In all the ages of man, God has searched for spiritual tradesmen to labor with Him. He has called them to faith and given them vision so they could complete their part of the plan. Even though they might not have known it, all of them have worked toward the end-goal of seeing Christ's throne established on the earth, in Jerusalem.

Although many have not seen the big picture or understood God's master plan, like sub-tradesmen, they have faithfully built the part assigned to them. In the end, there will be a throne set up in a new world, and the earth will be filled with the glory of the Lord and those who have been faithful will be rewarded. Abraham, the father of the faith, was one of those builders.

Scripture says, *"By faith Abraham, when he was called to go to a place he would later receive as an inheritance, obeyed and went, even though he did not know where he was going... He was looking forward to the city with foundations, whose architect and builder is God." Heb. 11:8,10*

Seven Steps

In this chapter, we cannot search out all the details, but we can give a basic overview of this plan. Here are seven simple steps that will help us see, what I believe, is in the heart of God. The end goal of these seven steps is the throne of God and of the Lamb being built in Jerusalem, on the Temple Mount (see Rev. 22:3). I have made each step start with the letter "P" to help us remember them.

Step One - A Plan

Sometime in eternity past, God had a plan. Before the foundations of the earth, all of these plans were established. For example, God chose His family in Christ before the foundations of the world. He chose His Son Jesus, and all who are saved in Christ are automatically chosen by God to be part of His new family. God has a plan for His family and a master plan for the earth and for the entire universe.

Step Two - A Planet

The Lord decided to position His throne in a new place (see Rev. 22:3), so He designed and created the best planet in the universe for this purpose. Earth is the unrivaled gem of the universe. It is the only planet, that scientists have discovered, that can possibly support a vast population of intelligent life.

But more than just supporting life, earth is spectacular. It has more fish species and more varieties of colorful birds than we can dream of. Some of the animals on earth have been privileged to be created in the image of heavenly creatures. Eagles, oxen, lions, and horses have been designed after spirit creatures that stand in the presence of God, before His throne.

John the revelator says he saw them in heaven (see Rev.5, 6, 19). They were not fashioned after earth's animals; on the contrary, they existed before the earth was made, so some earth animals were designed to look like them.

The complexities and creative details of animals on earth are found nowhere else in the universe.

Why? Because God has designed this planet for His throne. The vegetation, idyllic scenery, and intricacies of the ecosystems of our planet are always causing scientists, and nonscientists alike, to be in awe and wonder.

If you planned and designed your home, without financial limitations, where would it be and what would it look like? God made earth to be His new headquarters. He designed it to be perfect for His purpose and pleasure.

Step Three - A Population

According to plan, God made His greatest creation; He created the human race. No other created thing is made in His image - not angels, or animals, or anything. God's finest creation is a human baby. He created us for fellowship with Him. He wanted an intelligent family, with His DNA, to be with Him in fellowship forever.

Scripture says, *"Now are we the children of God, and what we will be has not yet been revealed. We know that when Christ appears, we will be like him, for we shall see him as he is." 1 Jn. 3:2*

He made the human population in His image but we are not yet complete. From the beginning, He designed a process to bring us to fullness. Through the cross of Christ and the infilling of His Holy Spirit we are changed even more. It is called salvation and sanctification. It comes through faith and obedience to Him. It starts when we believe, but continues as we cooperate with the Spirit of God who is working in us (see Philippians 2:12). The sanctification process will be completed when Christ returns to earth to set up His throne in Jerusalem. Our perfection and glorification arrive on resurrection day.

Step Four - A Person

From before the foundations of the earth, God chose Abraham to be the example of faith. He comes from the lineage of Noah and Shem, and his lineage continues all the way to Christ.

When we look at Abraham's life, we receive an education. He was tested by God, and through it He learned to walk by faith. His ultimate faith test was to offer Isaac, his son, on the altar of sacrifice. He passed the test and God spared his son, and provided a lamb in place of Isaac.

That lamb was a foreshadow of Christ, who is the Lamb of God. Abraham became the father of the faithful, and according to the master plan, he became the grandfather of Israel, God's chosen people.

Step Five - A Chosen People

The Bible calls the Jews, "God's chosen people" (see Deut. 14:2). They were chosen before the foundations of the earth because God wanted a people who would serve Him around His throne. They will host God's international family who will come from the nations to Jerusalem for the feasts of the Lord (see Zech. 14:16).

In the New Testament, Paul says eight things about the Jews. These eight things describe the complete destiny that God planned for His chosen people. Paul says, *"Theirs is the <u>adoption to sonship</u>; theirs the <u>divine glory</u>, the <u>covenants</u>, the <u>receiving of the law</u>, the <u>temple worship</u> and the <u>promises</u>. Theirs are the <u>patriarchs</u>, and from them is traced the <u>human ancestry of the Messiah</u>, who is God over all, forever praised! Amen." Rom. 9:4-5* (Emphasis added)

The Jews are special. Their forefathers are the heroes of the Bible. They gave us the teachings and stories of the Bible, and Jesus is the main story. He was a Jew.

The Jews will be used of God in a special role when Jesus comes to earth and rules from the temple mount. It is important that we honor and bless them.

Step Six - The Prince of Heaven

From beginning to end, Jesus Christ is the light, life, and salvation of the world. He is God, and at the same time, He is the Son of God. He is the Prince of Heaven. In Him we live and move and have our being. Everything was made by Him and is held together through Him. He is the Savior of the world.

From before the foundations of the earth, it was planned that Christ would die for us. He is the Truth, the Life and the Way. He died to take away our sins and we are forever saved through Him. In all things, He will always have the preeminence. He is the King of kings and the Lord of lords.

Even in heaven, He retains His Jewish identity. He is still called the Lion from the tribe of Judah and the Root of David (see Rev. 5:5).

Step Seven - A Place

On this gorgeous planet, God preordained a throne site. It is the temple mount in Jerusalem. It is the center of the world. Some go so far as to call it the navel of the earth.

This is God's special place and He has put His name here. Looking down from the sky, one can actually see the Hebrew letter Shin in the topography of the land around the temple mount. Shin stands for the name Shaddai, which is one of the names of God. He carved His name in the earth at the place where He purposed to set His throne. As previously stated, Jerusalem is special because it is destined for God's throne. From before the foundation of the world, this place was chosen for this purpose.

Scripture says, *"But you are to seek the place the LORD your God will choose from among all your tribes to put his Name there for his dwelling. To that place you must go"..."Be careful not to sacrifice your burnt offerings anywhere you please." Deut. 12:5,13*

The temple mount in Jerusalem is the place where God has put His name forever. It is part of the main focus of His eternal plan.

The Zeal of The Lord

Scripture tells us that God's plans are from everlasting to everlasting and they cannot be stopped (see Ps. 90:1-2). That means they reach back in eternity before the earth was created, and stretch forward into eternity future further than anything we can know. His plans are from everlasting to everlasting.

So, we can see God's big picture beginning to unfold— it includes His plan, a planet, a population, a special person, a chosen people, a Prince of heaven, and an appointed place. When we look at the world today we may ask ourselves how God's plans can possibly be completed. The answer, however, is clear, "The zeal of the Lord will accomplish this."

"Of the greatness of his government and peace there will be no end... from that time on and forever. <u>The zeal of the LORD Almighty will accomplish this</u>." Isa. 9:7 (Emphasis added)

Zeal is defined as, *"Great energy or enthusiasm in pursuit of a cause."*

God's enthusiasm is the greatest force in the universe. If He decides to do something, nothing can stop it.

Scripture says, *"People swear by something greater than themselves, and an oath confirms what is said and puts an end to all argument. Because God wanted to make the <u>unchanging nature of his purpose</u> clear to the heirs of what was promised, he confirmed it with an oath." Heb. 6:16-17* (Emphasis added)

A great part of God's eternal plan is His temple mount in Jerusalem. In the next chapter, we will explore more details regarding the preparation of God's holy city.

CHAPTER FOUR

The Foundation Stone

Bible Threads

If you want to understand a doctrine of the Bible, start by looking up every verse on the subject. Then weave the verses together like threads in a garment. Do it in such a way that the verses do not contradict each other. If they contradict each other, you don't have the correct doctrine yet. Work at all of the possibilities until all of the verses can be explained in harmony and without contradiction. Then, and only then, do you have the correct doctrine on the subject.

Often students of scripture take one or two verses and make a doctrine out of them. That is dangerous. That process is the mother of error and false teaching.

Scripture says, *"Study to shew thyself approved unto God, a workman that needeth not to be ashamed, rightly dividing the word of truth." 2 Tim. 2:15 KJV*

The process of diligently searching the scriptures reveals God's plans. From one end of His word to the other, the same truth will show up time and again. His purpose is woven together so that it becomes evident to those who search for it.

The Foundation Stone in Jerusalem

When we look at Jerusalem, the place that God chose for His throne, we discover that it shows up time and again in the Bible. It appears in Genesis, Revelation, in the books of the Kings, the Prophets, and the Gospels.

As mentioned earlier, Jerusalem has several names. It is Mount Moriah, Mount Zion, Salem, the Temple Mount, the Mountain of the Lord's Temple, the threshing floor, the Lord Will Provide, and the place where God has put His name. Some people call it, the place of the foundation stone.

It is ground zero and the eyes of the Lord are focused on it. From the beginning, it's as though the spotlight of heaven has shone upon this place and its special foundation rock. Look at how God wove the threads of His purpose to emphasize its importance.

"For the Lord has chosen Zion, he has desired it for his dwelling, saying, "This is my resting place forever

and ever; here I will sit enthroned, for I have desired it." Ps. 132:13-14

God chose the temple mount in Jerusalem; He will rule from there. He has desired it and made it His resting place forever. Here are seven things that will help us to further recognize the importance of Jerusalem. First, we will look at some Bible threads and discover five of the most important events in history. All of them happened at this place. Then, we will look at two other events, which many Jewish theologians believe also happened at this site. You can decide for yourself if you think these last two events should be included with the first five that we find in Scripture.

Rather than start from the beginning, we will start at the end and work our way backward. We will do a historical countdown from event seven to event one. I trust you will realize the amazing significance of Jerusalem.

Event Seven - The Throne

In this historical list, number seven is Christ's throne being positioned on the temple mount in Jerusalem. It is still in the future. When Jesus returns He will strike down the kingdom of darkness and establish His throne. I believe it will rest on the foundation stone, on the temple mount. From there, He will rule the nations.

Water will flow from under the throne, and everywhere it goes it will bring forth life - even down to the Dead Sea (see Ezek. 47:9). Worshippers will come to Jerusalem to worship the Lord, and from there, His glory will cover the earth. Jerusalem will vibrate with life, and people will stream from the nations to the temple mount to see the King and celebrate the feasts. The impartation of Christ's government and grace will bring continual prosperity to the world. Without a doubt, the most important event that happens on the foundation stone is the setting up of the throne for the rule of King Jesus.

We read: *"At that time <u>they will call Jerusalem The Throne of the LORD</u>, and all nations will gather in Jerusalem to honor the name of the LORD. No longer will they follow the stubbornness of their evil hearts." Jer. 3:17* (Emphasis added)

To me, it is obvious that this Scripture speaks of physical nations whose representatives will gather on the temple mount, in a physical Jerusalem, in the land of Israel.

Event Six - The Crucifixion and Resurrection

Moving backward in time, here is the next event: the judgment, crucifixion, and resurrection of Christ, which happened within a few hundred yards of the foundation stone, on the temple mount.

Antonia's fortress was on the temple mount. That is where Pilate had Christ flogged, tortured, and judged before the people. From there, Jesus carried His cross a short distance out of the city gate to Golgotha, the crucifixion site. In that same place, there was a garden where Jesus was placed in a tomb, and from there He rose from the grave.

It all happened on Mount Moriah, God's chosen mountain. It is the Mountain of the Lord's Temple. These events and the precise location of them are recorded in the last chapters of all four gospels - Matthew, Mark, Luke and John. This is so significant. The passion of Christ and the actions that brought about the salvation of the human race took place here.

Event Five - The Temple

Reaching back even further in history we discover event number five. It took place in the time of King Solomon. The temple was built around the foundation stone on the temple mount.

David's son built it according to the pattern in heaven, and it was built to house the ark of the covenant and bring the presence and glory of God to the people of earth. When it was dedicated, fire came down from heaven and lit the sacrifice. This happened during the Feast of Tabernacles.

Then, the Lord appeared to Solomon in the night and told him that this place was a place for meeting with God. Even if people were in another nation but faced this place and walked uprightly, God would hear their prayers, deliver them, and prosper them (see 2 Chr. 6:38).

"When Solomon finished the temple of the Lord... the Lord appeared to him at night and said, "I have heard your prayer and <u>have chosen this place for myself</u>"..."When I shut up the heavens so that there is no rain, or command locusts to devour the land or send a plague among my people, <u>if my people, who are called by my name, will humble themselves and pray and seek my face and turn from their wicked ways, then I will hear from heaven, and I will forgive their sin and heal their land.</u> Now my eyes will be open and my ears will be attentive to the prayers offered <u>in this place</u>. <u>I have chosen and consecrated this place so that my Name may be there forever. My eyes and my heart will always be there</u>. " 2 Chr. 7:11-16 (Emphasis added)

The temple being built on this site was God's provision. He says that His eyes and heart will always be there. This is the site of the present day temple mount. God chose this place and consecrated it for Himself, and His name will be there forever.

Event Four - The Threshing Floor

We are learning that the Jerusalem site is a major part of the plans of God. Before the temple was built,

God told David to purchase the site from Araunah the Jebusite. David conquered the city of Jebu, but he sinned, and God judged him and the nation. David repented, and God sent him to the threshing floor of Araunah. I am confident that this was at the highest point of land on Mount Moriah. It was above the city of Jebu, which was later called Jerusalem. On Araunah's threshing floor was God's foundation stone. We read about the threshing floor in the following verses:

"On that day Gad went up to David and said to him, "Go up and build an altar to the LORD on the threshing floor of Araunah the Jebusite." So David went up as the Lord had commanded through Gad... Araunah said, "Why has my lord the king come to his servant?" "To buy your threshing floor," David answered, "So I can build an altar to the Lord, that the plague on the people may be stopped." Araunah said to David, "Let my lord the king take whatever he wishes"... But the king replied to Araunah, "No, I insist on paying you for it." So David bought the threshing floor and the oxen and paid fifty shekels of silver for them... David built an altar to the Lord there and sacrificed... And the Lord answered his prayer... and the plague on Israel was stopped." 2 Sam. 24:18-25

Although, at the time, David did not know it, he actually bought Araunah's threshing floor in preparation for the future building of the temple and the establishment of a throne room for King Jesus. It was part of God's master plan that had been established from before the foundations of the earth. David and Solomon were co-laborers with God for the unfolding this plan.

Event Three - Abraham's Sacrifice

This is amazing. A thousand years before King David lived, the site of the Temple Mount was barren. There was no city or people living there. At that time, God told Abraham to take his son Isaac and offer him up as a sacrifice on Mount Moriah. It was later called the Mountain of the Lord.

Abraham traveled for three days and then he saw a bald rock, a mountain sticking up in the middle of a circle of other mountains. And God said, "That's the place." So Abraham went down into the Kidron valley and climbed the steep mountain with his son. What followed took place at the exact spot where the temple would later stand. I believe, Abraham's sacrifice happened on the foundation stone. Let us read what took place.

"God said, "'Take your son, your only son, Isaac, whom you love, and go to the region of Moriah. Sacrifice him there as a burnt offering on <u>one of the mountains I will tell you about</u>.'" ... On the third day Abraham looked up and saw the place at a distance... When they reached the place <u>God had told him about</u>, Abraham built an altar...But the angel of the Lord called out to him from heaven... 'Do not lay a hand

on the boy.' ... Abraham looked up and there in the thicket he saw a ram... He went over and took the ram and sacrificed it as a burnt offering instead of his son. So <u>Abraham called the place, The Lord Will Provide</u>. And to this day it is said, 'On the mountain of the Lord it will be provided.'" Gen. 22:2-14 (Emphasis added)

The mountaintop that God led Abraham to, was called, The Lord will Provide. It was not only the place where God provided a lamb in place of Isaac, it became the Temple Mount where God's provision flowed from the temple. It also became the place where He provided salvation through the cross of Christ and where, in the future, He will provide His throne of government.

Abraham believed that God would raise his son from the dead if he were killed (see Heb. 11:19). Instead of killing Isaac, God provided a ram to take Isaac's place. I believe the lamb was sacrificed on the rock that protruded up from the top of the mountain. I believe that Isaac had been laid on God's foundation stone.

Two thousand years later, God provided another Lamb. It was His Son Jesus, the Lamb of God, who came to take our place and pay for our sins. The crucifixion of Jesus happened in Jerusalem, on the same mountain. This is Mount Moriah, the temple mount, the place that Christ chose and designed for His throne.

The final two events involving the foundation stone are what many Jews believe. You can decide for yourself if you think these proposals are legitimate.

Event Two - The Making of Adam

Although it would be difficult to substantiate from Scripture, it is believed by many Jewish theologians that the site of the foundation stone is where mankind was created. They say that God made Adam from the dust of the earth and that dirt came from this place. You may or may not believe it, but it is possible.

God systematically incorporates layers of importance in everything He does. He weaves the threads of His plans together so that His greatness can be seen both in the big picture and also in the smallest details.

It certainly makes sense for God to create man at the site of this hot spot. This place and all that it represents is the reason He created the planet. He wants everything to point to the place where He has put His name, the place where His throne will be.

Event One - The Creation of Earth

The seven-fold countdown leads us to the dawn of creation. It is believed by many Jews, although we cannot substantiate it or find it in the Bible, that the earth was created around the foundation stone. The thought stretches our imagination. We certainly cannot make a doctrine out of this idea, but it may be true.

These theologians do not believe that some earthquake, or pushing together of earth's plates, caused Mount Moriah and its foundation stone to rise. They believe, rather, that God made the foundation stone and built the rest of the world around it.

Can you picture Him designing the foundation stone? They believe it was a rock that He created and hurled into space. Then, He formed particles and stuck them to the foundation stone. He continued the process by spinning it on its axis and putting it in orbit around the sun until the planet took its circular shape and earth was formed. It is certainly different from any other planet that man has discovered so far.

Undeniable Evidence

Whether or not you believe the last two events and their Jerusalem placement, it is undeniable that Jerusalem is God's chosen place here on earth. This is confirmed again and again, by the teachings and threads of Scripture.

CHAPTER FIVE

The Ark of the Covenant

Immanuel

In this chapter we will talk about the all-important ark of the covenant, but before we get to it, I will present a brief explanation to give us some context.

Immanuel means, 'God with us', or 'God dwelling with us'. That is what the ark is all about. In its time, it brought the presence of God to mankind. It was a foreshadowing of Jesus, who is Immanuel.

"The virgin will conceive and give birth to a son, and they will call him Immanuel" (which means 'God with us')." Mt. 1:23

God being with us is central to His plan. He says, ***"My dwelling place will be with them; I will be their God, and they will be my people." Ezek. 37:27***

The Lord has revealed Himself to mankind through different means and with different levels of intensity. He came to us by speaking though holy men of old. He came through the scriptures, through the apostles and even through the appearance of angels. His dwelling with us is designed to be more intimate with every passing age. We will discover how the ark of the covenant fits into this picture. It is one way that He came and dwelt among us. The ark revealed God's glory. It was a holy, Immanuel item.

Immanuel and God's Family

In the Garden of Eden, the Lord walked and talked with Adam and Eve. He wanted a family to share His life and His love with. He was, and still is, looking for a rich and meaningful level of fellowship. That is why we are His children and He is our Father. A good father does not just create children; he wants to interact with them.

In order to bring forth such a great family, a process has been set in place. We have already been gifted with the ability to create and invent that which is beyond ourselves, and that is necessary for rich fellowship. Man's inventive dynamic continues to develop but the Lord is also looking for another important quality. He wants more than just an intelligent family, He wants one with moral character, one that possesses His virtue and love. He created man for His pleasure. He is looking for good, glorious, dynamic fellowship.

God's character, flowing in us, will produce righteousness, peace, and joy. Our goal is to be like Jesus and without that goal, our interaction with God will not be harmonious, enjoyable, or productive. We were fearfully and wonderfully made in His image and we are not robots; He gave us the right to choose.

In order for God to give us choice, He shows us what options lay before us. It seems that not everyone is interested, but those who search for Him, will find Him. Those who hunger and thirst for the right ways of the Lord will be filled and satisfied beyond measure.

Ultimately, that is why Jesus, God's Son, came and lived among us. He showed us His glory. He is Immanuel, God with us.

Rebellion

Let us delve deeper into the Immanuel dynamic. We mentioned that God does not want to fellowship with machines or robots that are void of free will. No life-giving creator would desire robots for a family. His creation must be autonomous and people must willingly choose God because of His love, greatness, and glory.

This free will, however, opens the door to more than godliness, it also allows for rebellion against one's Creator. Rebellion is both commonplace and destructive. It was foreseen before the creation of the world and is another reason why the Son of God came to earth. He came to die for our sins.

Scripture says, *"We all, like sheep, have gone astray, each of us has turned to our own way; and the Lord has laid on him* [Jesus] *the iniquity of us all." Isa. 53:6*

The Jewish Example

God's interaction with His chosen people points to the fellowship He is looking for. The Jews were commissioned with a few tasks. For example, in the future, they will host the nations who come to Jerusalem to worship the King. People from around the world will come up to Zion for the amazing temple worship. The Bible speaks of the Jews in this regard. It says, **"Theirs is...the temple worship." Rom. 9:4** (see also Zech. 14:16).

In the millennium, the Jews will host the temple worship. They have another task as well; their lives have been examples that God used to teach the world His ways. Throughout history, the success and failure of the Jews are the results of how well they have listened and obeyed the Lord. In many ways, they have not done well.

The nations have seen the Jewish example as presented in the Bible. Everyone should learn from those examples. To help us with the learning process, both Jews and Gentiles are called to be disciples. History reveals that the Jews were the first people to become disciples of Christ.

Long before the coming of Jesus, the Jewish patriarchs, and later the Jewish apostles, became examples for us. They also became our instructors. The family of God is built upon the foundation stones of the apostles' teachings (see Rev. 21:4). I suggest to you, that much of what Scripture refers to as 'the apostle's doctrine' (see Acts 2:42), is highlighted in the book of Hebrews. Hebrews teaches us ten new doctrines that are better than what the Jews were given under the Old Covenant. Those ten teachings are the backbone of the apostles; doctrine.

God Comes to Us Through the Bible

Part of God's plan was the creation of the Bible. In it we discover the plan of salvation, the journey of man, and the ancient history of the Jews. In fact, the Bible is used as a textbook for history classes in Israel. The whole world should be wiser because of the examples they left us in the Scriptures. It has been said, *"A wise man learns from his mistakes, but a wiser man learns from someone else's mistakes."* (Author unknown)

We should learn from the mistakes and from the successes that the Jews have made.

Scripture says, *"Do not grumble, as some of them did - and were killed by the destroying angel. <u>These things happened to them as examples</u> and were written down as warnings for us, on whom the culmination of the ages has come." 1 Cor. 10:10-11* (Emphasis added)

The examples and teachings of the Jews are evident. The Bible was created for the whole world; it belongs to all people. It is also a book about God and the Jews. In fact the Jews are called, "The People of the Book."

God Comes in a Number of Ways

We are talking about the ways that God is with us, and the Bible is one of those ways. God commissioned the Jews to write the Bible. In it we find the principles that God expects us to live by. It is the greatest tool we have ever received. It is the manual for life and, in a way, it has brought God to us. Even so, God gives us more than the Bible.

The Lord also gives us miracles. His plan for man's progress is methodical and it is full of spiritual intervention. He often interacts with us on a supernatural level, and that produces amazing testimonies.

The Lord also comes to us in the lives of people. He gave us the heroes of the Bible and other outstanding individuals who were filled with the Holy Spirit. In spite of the fact that all humans fail, many have demonstrated great virtue. According to plan, God has raised up heroes who live exemplary lives of courage and godliness.

The Ark

The story of God dwelling with man is a phenomenon. After He walked with Adam and Eve in the garden, they disobeyed and were separated from Him. Then, the Lord spoke through holy men of old and they delivered His word to the people.

"Prophecy never had its origin in the human will, but prophets, though human, spoke from God as they were carried along by the Holy Spirit." 2 Pet. 1:21

Eventually, Jesus and the Holy Spirit came, but before their coming, God gave us the ark of the covenant. It was the first example of God's abiding presence, since the Garden of Eden.

The Lord said, *"Make a sanctuary for me, and I will dwell among them." Ex. 25:8*

The most important piece of furniture in the sanctuary was the ark of the covenant. It was covered in gold, and on top of it were two cherubim with their wings stretched over the mercy seat. God spoke to the high priest of Israel from above the mercy seat. It was a foreshadowing of Jesus' throne and His presence abiding with us.

The Ark in the Wilderness

For forty years, the Israelites travelled through the wilderness and they carried the ark with them. A cloud rose from the ark by day and a pillar of fire rose from it by night. The fire and cloud were so massive and they rose so high that they warmed two million people in the nights and shadowed them from the heat of the sun by day.

Inside the ark were three items that pointed to the coming of Jesus. They were manna (the bread that was eaten in the wilderness), the stone tablets of the Ten Commandments, and the budding almond branch that belonged to Aaron, the High Priest.

1. <u>Manna</u> represented Christ, because He is the bread of life that came down from heaven.

2. <u>The Ten Commandments</u> represented Christ, because He is the Word of God.

3. <u>Aaron's rod</u> that budded points to Christ, because the rod represented the authority and commissioning of the high priest. Jesus is our great high priest.

The Ark Comes to Zion

The tabernacle in the wilderness finally rested in Gibeon (see 1 Chr. 16:39). It took another four hundred and forty years before the temple was made and the ark of the covenant was placed in it, on the

The Ark of the Covenant

temple mount. Above the ark, the presence of God rested with the human race.

Before the ark was brought to the temple mount, the people of Israel went astray. At one point, their rebellion was so bad that the Lord allowed the Philistines to steal the ark and put it in their pagan temple.

This was a catastrophic mistake for the Philistines. The idols of their false gods came crashing down and the people were struck with plagues of mice and they were afflicted with hemorrhoids. They could not get rid of the ark quick enough, so they sent it back to Israel on a cart.

Unfortunately, the Israelites adopted this method of moving the ark. Instead of employing God's prescribed way, they moved it on an oxen cart. The priests had been commissioned by God to carry the ark, but the Israelites did not obey the Lord.

As the ark was being moved on the cart, Uzzah tried to steady it, when the oxen who pulled it stumbled. He was instantly killed and it took 20 years for David to finally bring the ark to Jerusalem, and put it in a tent behind the palace.

After his son, Solomon, built the temple, the ark finally found its resting place on Mount Zion. I believe it was placed on the foundation stone. That was its preordained place according to God's great plan.

The ark represents the presence of God and the rule of Christ. Its assigned resting place was determined before the earth was ever created. It was destined for the Temple Mount.

Christ, the Church, and the Ark

The ark was a foreshadowing of Jesus Christ and His coming rule on the Temple Mount. It was a long and arduous journey that brought it to the sanctuary of the Lord.

God's Immanuel plan will culminate with the Lord Jesus enthroned at this site. I believe that His throne will be set on that same stone where the ark was placed. The ark had to be brought there because it represented the presence of God dwelling with man. A cloud rose from it by day and a fire by night. It presented a picture of the future covering and blessings of Jesus over all humanity.

The ark could not be brought to Jerusalem on an ox cart. It had to come to its resting place according to God's plan. It had to be carried by the priests. In corresponding manner, Jesus will come to mount Zion in God's way, and at His appointed time. Apostles and prophets, filled with the Holy Spirit, will carry the revelation and usher in the return of the King.

The Rule of Christ

The Lord's rule is unstoppable, but other things must first line up with God's plan. The Church must come to holiness and greatness, and the people of Israel must return to the God of Abraham through Jesus the Messiah.

A Holy Spirit revival will come to Israel and a massive revival will invigorate the nations. These revivals will precede the coming of the King (see my books <u>Unexpected Fire</u> and <u>Israel's Coming Revival</u>).

The Lord says, *"My dwelling place will be with them; I will be their God, and they will be my people." Ezek. 37:27*

The ark was part of God's master plan. It points to His Son. He will have His family, His world, and His universe. Whatever you do, no matter what the cost, make sure that you and your family are part of God's great plan. This is your inheritance. It is the blessing that God has promised His people.

The Apostle Peter said, *"To this you were called, so that you might inherit a blessing." 1 Pet. 3:9*

PART TWO

Who is Man That You Are Mindful of Him

CHAPTER SIX

The Journey of Man

The Fullness of Christ

The whole world will one day be the Church. When God is finished transforming the human race, everyone on the planet will be part of Jesus' body. We will all be called the Bride of Christ, the fullness of Him who fills all in all. We will be the nations of the saved and the family of God. Along with angels and the unknown of the universe, we will be God's kingdom dwelling in unity and righteousness.

I believe the government of the universe will emanate from earth. More to the point, it will come from the city of Jerusalem. As previously stated, that is where the thrones of God and of the Lamb will be (see Rev. 22:1-5).

Sharing His Glory

It makes perfect sense that God would create humanity; He wants fellowship. Like most of us, He wants a family. We are made in His image, so it is not that God thinks like us, but rather, we tend to think like Him. Most of us really like having a family.

It also makes sense that His plan includes a process that leads us from great beginnings to an even greater glory. We start off being made in His image, and in the future we are told that we will be partakers of His glory. Glory describes everything that is great about God.

Scripture says, *"We are heirs - heirs of God and co-heirs with Christ, if indeed we share in his sufferings ... <u>we may also share in his glory</u>." Rom. 8:17* (Emphasis added)

Receiving God's glory is about sharing God's greatness. I have heard some Bible teachers wrongly preach that God will not share His glory with people.

They get this idea from the Scripture that says, *"I will not yield my glory to another or my praise to idols." Isa. 42:8*

The context of the verse tells us that God will not share His glory with another so-called god. He will not share His glory with an idol or a demon. The

Bible, however, repeatedly tells us that God *will* share His glory with His sons and daughters. In fact, Jesus died to bring many sons into glory (see Heb. 2:10).

God's Plan is Bigger

God's plan for people is bigger than what we might think. In Himself, God has everything but He still wants a family. The Bible says that we will become His fullness when we become His family. My family is my fullness and so it will be with God. We are complete in Him and He is complete in us. Our spiritual eyes need to be opened so that we can see this great revelation.

"I pray that the eyes of your heart may be enlightened in order that you may know the hope to which he has called you, the riches of <u>his glorious inheritance in his holy people</u>." Eph. 1:18 (Emphasis added)

That thought is incredible. The gap between where we are, and where God has planned for us to be, seems insurmountable.

Scripture says, *"And God placed all things under his* [Jesus'] *feet and appointed him to be head over everything for the church, which is his body, <u>the fullness of him who fills everything in every way</u>." Eph. 1:22-23* (Emphasis added)

How can this be? How can we be the fullness of God? What kind of transformation will this require? The human race, ultimately the church, cannot rise to such grandeur without embarking on an amazing preordained journey. This is an essential part of God's master plan.

Milestones on Our Journey

Here are fourteen milestones of God's provision for the human race. Some of this presentation will be a review of what has already been taught. Each milestone from the past, and some that are still ahead, are part of God's great plan.

1. Milestone number one is the creation of man in God's image. *"So God created mankind in his own image, in the image of God he created them; male and female he created them." Gen. 1:27*

2. Milestone two involves teaching man to pray and call on the name of the Lord. *"Seth [Adam's son] had a son, and he named him Enosh. At that time people began to call on the name of the Lord." Gen. 4:26*

3. Milestone number three is the Holy Spirit speaking through holy men of old. *"...in old times... holy men of God spake as they were moved by the Holy Ghost." 2 Pet. 1:21 KJV*

4. Milestone four is the raising up of a chosen people. The Jews were created and chosen as the Lord's treasured possession, and to be a banner for the nations. Concerning the Jews, we read, *"You are the children of the Lord your God"..."for you are a people*

holy to the Lord your God. Out of all the peoples on the face of the earth, the Lord has <u>chosen you to be his treasured possession</u>." Deut.14:1-2. (Emphasis added) (see also Deut. 7:14).

"He will raise a banner for the nations and gather the exiles of Israel." Isa. 11:12

5. Milestone five is the giving of the Law to show us God's expectations. *"These commandments that I give you today are to be on your hearts. Impress them on your children." Deut. 6:6*

6. Milestone number six is the gift of the ark of the covenant. *"I will meet with you: and from above the mercy seat, from between the two cherubim which are upon the ark of the testimony, I will speak to you." Ex. 25:22 NAS*

7. Milestone number seven is the birth of Jesus the Messiah, the Son of God. *"But when the set time had fully come, God sent his Son." Gal. 4:4*

8. Milestone number eight is the gift of salvation through faith in Christ Jesus to bring us into the family of God. *"Jesus is... the cornerstone. Salvation is found in no one else, for there is no name under heaven given to mankind by which we must be saved." Acts 4:11-12*

9. Milestone number nine is the gift of God's Holy Spirit, the down payment of our inheritance. This gift was given on the day of Pentecost. *"...wait for the gift my Father promised...For John baptized with water, but in a few days you will be baptized with the Holy*

Spirit... you shall receive power when the Holy Spirit comes on you..." Acts 1:4-5,8

"The Holy Spirit is the down payment of our inheritance." Eph. 1:14 CS

10. Milestone number ten is sanctification through the indwelling work of the Holy Spirit and the process of discipleship. *"It is God's will that you should be sanctified." 1 Thes. 4:3*

"Work out your salvation with fear and trembling, for it is God who works in you to will and act in order to fulfill his good purpose." Phil. 2:12-13

11. Milestone eleven is the emergence of the church. *"I will build my church and the gates of Hades will not overcome it." Mt. 16:18*

12. Milestone number twelve is the invitation for us to serve in partnership with Christ. It starts now and continues in eternity. *"The throne of God and of the Lamb will be in the city, and <u>his servants will serve him</u>." Rev. 22:3* (Emphasis added)

13. Milestone thirteen is the second coming of Christ. At that time we are made like Christ. It is the completion and fullness of the church. *"For the Lord himself will come down from heaven...and the dead in Christ will rise first. After that, we who are still alive and are left will be caught up together with them in the clouds to meet the Lord in the air." 1 Thes. 4:16-17*

"Now we are the children of God, and what we will be has not yet been made known. But we know that

when Christ appears, we shall be like him, for we shall see him as he is." 1 Jn. 3:2

14. Milestone number fourteen is reigning with Christ. *"This is a trustworthy saying: If we died with him, we shall also live with him. If we endure we shall also reign with him. 2 Tim. 2:11-12*

"You have made them to be a kingdom and priests to serve our God, and they will reign on the earth." Rev. 5:10

Seven of these milestones happened before the death of Christ and seven happen after His death. The fourteen milestones of humanity take the human race from great beginnings (being made in the image of God) to being the fullness of Him who fills everything in every way (God's family). In Christ, the full provision is available to all but we must embrace it. That is true for every generation, whether we refer to those who came before us, or for those generations still to come.

Steps of a Good Man

Choosing and learning to walk with the Lord requires humility and obedience. The journey of man must line up with the plans of God. Though we choose well and walk well, every one of us will fall short of the glory of God at some time. The Lord has even made provision for our ongoing failures.

As the Lord compensates for our stumbling, He looks at our hearts. He looks to see if we will delight in Him. When He finds a person whose heart delights in the Lord, He supports them, redeems them, and perfects them. He does that with everyone who will humble themselves and have faith.

Scripture says, *"The Lord makes firm the steps of the one who delights in him; though he may stumble, he will not fall, for the Lord upholds him with his hand." Ps. 37:23-24*

Overcoming Failures

Being a pastor for more than fifty years has shown me a lot of human weakness. Everyone I know has failed in some way. The amazing thing is that the grace of God carries and restores all who trust and obey Him.

It is easy, at times, to become discouraged with our lack of progress. Others may bring distraction to themselves and to those under their care. They do this because they do not understand the big picture and may therefore get bogged down in the weeds. Some may even lose their way, as they strain at a gnat and swallow a camel. They can do this by focusing hard on legalisms and minute details (see Mt. 23:24).

Getting Caught In The Weeds

Unless we see enough of God's plan, we are bound to get caught in the weeds. When fishing, a fisherman does not want to get caught in the weeds. If his hook gets entangled in the grasses, he has to stop fishing. He must turn off his boat engine, go backward and try to untangle the mess. He might spent all of his time working the weeds and never fulfill the end-goal of fishing.

Many saints get caught in the weeds; they love the Lord, worship Him, study His word, and share His love, but still do not have a kingdom perspective. They are in the lake but not partnering with the end-time purpose of God. They are spending a lot of time and energy at the edges where all the weeds are. They may be striving to build their own kingdom but not see and understand the Lord's kingdom.

That is the work of pride. When pride surfaces, people will either get caught in the sins of the world or the sins of religious self-righteousness. No matter what side they fall off the bike, it remains the same: pride will hinder their progress.

Thank God that our failure is not the end of the story because God has given us the gift of eternal life through the death of His Son on the cross. We can have lots of pride, wrong doctrine, and even poor behavior, yet by God's grace, we can still make it to heaven.

Scripture says, ***"The wages of sin is death, <u>but the gift of God is eternal life through Jesus Christ our Lord</u>." Rom. 6:23*** (Emphasis added)

Help For My Personal Journey

I am constantly surprised by the push and pull of the Lord's call on my life. Like you, I am on a journey to take hold of the prize that God has called me to. Though I do not do this perfectly, I am continually brought to the burning bush (the place where God speaks) and when I look at the flames, God speaks to me and I follow. The direction He has me travel, always seems to be upstream and against the flow. One thing I am sure of, the Lord will complete His plan, and bring me to His ultimate purpose. The zeal of the Lord will do this; He upholds me in His hands.

Reach For As Much As You Can

Here we are, between eternity past and eternity future. We can only know as much as the Lord reveals to us. Regardless of the depth of our revelation, our faith should be intense and our attitudes and behavior should follow our faith. If we obey the revelation and the direction the Lord extends to us, He will give us more. I have learned from personal experience that if I do my best, He will do the rest.

CHAPTER SEVEN

Why The Church?

Together

The Church is a definitive part of God's plan. By being an active part of the Church, we have an opportunity to learn and experience His purpose, and walk according to His plan? It is the place where we can practice being the family that God wants us to be. Can the human race be the Church that God Has designed? Christ's coming kingdom will consist of love, service, righteousness, peace and joy. One day, all will be under His authority. The Church, empowered with His authority, will produce His plan. We will be His family, but we need practice.

When we celebrate the Lord's Supper we remember what Christ did for us on the cross, but in the

Communion Scripture, we also see the importance of the Church. We are warned to discern and appreciate each other when receiving the elements or we could become sick and even die. The Church is a serious matter to God, because Jesus died to bring it forth. He insists that it should function like a family.

"Everyone ought to examine themselves before they eat of the bread and drink from the cup. For those who eat and drink without discerning the body of Christ [the Church] *eat and drink judgment on themselves. That is why many among you are weak and sick, and a number of you have fallen asleep." 1 Cor. 11:28-30*

Only One Church

There is really only one Church in the whole world, but the function and interaction of the church members cannot be worked out from a distance. Love and unity cannot be shared, in a tangible way, with someone on the other side of the world.

The Church finds reality and meaning in community congregations. On the local scene, together with other members of God's family, we do two things - we share His love, and communicate His truth to the world around us. We, the Church, are the pillar and ground of God's truth. We hold to His ways and demonstrate them for all to see.

Scripture says, "[This is] *God's household; which is the church of the living God, the pillar and foundation of the truth."* 1Tim. 3:15

Defining the Church

Before continuing, we should explain what the Church is, and what it is not. The Church is not a building, although many in our modern world refer to a building that is used for Christian services as a church. The Church is not even all of the people who attend weekly meetings in such a building, for some who attend might not be genuine followers of Christ. The Church is the community of genuine Christians. Christians are people who, in word and deed, have become followers of Christ.

A Christian is a person who has believed that Jesus died on the cross for them, has repented of their sins, called on His name, and confessed Him as Lord. The Bible says that those people are saved and born again by God's Spirit. The Church is all people who have followed that plan and taken those steps.

The local church is all people in a specific congregation, who have become saved by believing in the Lord Jesus and by taking those steps. Like the thief on the cross, they are accepted by the Lord, even though their past may be terrible. They do not have to be perfect or mature to go to heaven.

The Seven Goals of Christ's Church

The Bible teaches us what the Church should be and what it should do. From my research, I have discovered seven main characteristics of a Bible church. If these are God's goals they will be appropriate for any congregation, in any country around the world. They should be goals that we aim for. These characteristics are not dependent on a specific culture, but can be embraced by all. We understand that the local church is made up of those who are saved and who gather together to worship the Lord. After salvation, people should press on to learn and do God's will. As I see it, the following is what they should aim for:

1. Goal number one for the church is to see everyone <u>become a disciple</u>. Given the fact that the church is made up of believers, the process of personal sanctification, growth, and obedience to Christ is vital.

A Christian disciple is one who is under the discipline of Christ. This requires the ability to hear God's voice - for how can you obey the Lord if you do not hear what He is saying? Seven ways that God speaks to us include: 1. Through the Bible, 2. Through the inner voice of the Holy Spirit, 3. Though other people, such as pastors and prophets, 4. Through signs and wonders, 5. Through dreams and visions, 6. Through angels, and 7. By the audible voice of God.

Any Christian who has faith will hear the Lord speaking to them through several of these ways. They will grow in faith as they read the Bible, worship, pray and obey the Lord.

2. Goal number two for the local church is to become a family. That means loving and serving one another. It involves encouraging and protecting one another and watching out for every church member's wellbeing. It means refusing gossip but bearing one another's burdens.

3. The third goal of a Bible church is to be a house of prayer. Jesus said, *"Is it not written: my house shall be called a house of prayer for all nations?" Mk. 11:17*

Individuals must learn to pray and whole congregations should pray with all kinds of prayers on all occasions (see Eph. 6:18).

Seven types of prayer that I have found in the Bible include: 1. Thanksgiving, 2. Dedication prayers, 3. Petitions, 4. Supplications, 5. Intercession, 6. Praise and Proclamations, and 7. Praying in Tongues,

4. The fourth goal of a Bible church is for everyone to become a minister. We want to see all people become believers, and all believers become disciples, and all disciples become ministers. Later in the book we will speak of apostles, prophets, evangelists, pastors and teachers. They are some of the ministers mentioned in the Bible, but there are also administrators, worship leaders, intercessors, encouragers,

givers, elders, deacons, mercy extenders, doorkeepers, ushers, and many others.

Ministers may serve in natural or supernatural ways, employing the gifts of miracles, faith, healings, discernment, wisdom, knowledge, tongues, prophecy, interpretation of tongues, and interpretation of prophecy. They may cast out demons, baptize new converts, or raise money to help the poor. God's people should minister in all of these ways, and that leads us to our next point.

5. Goal number five for a Bible church is to <u>care for widows, orphans, immigrants, handicapped people, and the poor</u>. This call to help disadvantaged people is found throughout the Scriptures. James tells us this is part of having pure religion before God (see Js. 1:27).

6. The sixth goal of a Bible church is to <u>be the light of the world</u>. We are not to hide our light under a bushel. The church should be a city set upon a hill so that all may see her good works and glorify her Father in heaven. Church members are called to be witnesses who bring many to salvation through Christ.

Being the light of the world means the church should also to be a prophetic voice in the nation. We should call individuals, families, and governments everywhere to a lifestyle of godliness, Christian charity and love.

7. The seventh goal of a Bible church is to <u>destroy the works of the devil</u>. Jesus came for this reason, and

we work for Him. Scripture says, *"The reason the Son of God appeared was to destroy the devil's work." 1 Jn. 3:8*

We are called to overcome evil with good. The devil comes to kill, steal, and destroy, but Jesus came to give us life. As we do the work of the ministry, we destroy the devil's foothold of destruction in people's lives.

Nothing is more satisfying than seeing someone taken from the kingdom of darkness and brought into the kingdom of God's dear Son. From that starting point, we teach, deliver, heal, and set the captives free. We destroy the devil's work by releasing the blessings of God.

A Church on Fire

The church on fire with the power of the Holy Spirit is a church full of love and miraculous testimonies. It is God's house, His hospital, His building, His training center, His body, His Bride and His family.

The Church, in this season, is not what it should be. It is not fulfilling the plans of God that we have mentioned in this chapter. The great lack that many see in today's Church has caused some to distance themselves from it. That is not the answer. All who see God's plan should be part of the solution and not the problem. It is time to work together for the glory of God. Independent and isolated Christians, even if they are gifted, may work against the plans of God because they do not discern and appreciate the Body of Christ appropriately. It takes humility to live and work and stay together.

Fellowship

The Church is where it all happens. It is in the redeemed community where the rough stones, at the proverbial bottom of the river, move together and bump along with each other until the rough edges of our lives get worn off. It involves some unintended friction. We could call that the process of fellowship. With genuine fellowship, each member becomes smoother and rounder so they may fly straighter for the ultimate purpose of the King. In other words, a disciple's character and calling is sharpened, to better serve the Lord, as they experience the relational interaction of the saints.

CHAPTER EIGHT

God's Government

All Authority

Besides the Trinity and the angelic hosts, people are assigned to be part of God's government. For this we need God's authority. The battle between light and darkness in the world is not intense for God; He has no worthy rivals. For every other being, however, the battle for life and godliness is intense.

Scripture says, *"For our struggle is not against flesh and blood, but against the rulers, against the authorities, against the powers of this dark world and against the spiritual forces of evil in the heavenly realms." Eph. 6:12*

Jesus is the Savior of the world and when He came, He demonstrated His power over everything.

He calmed storms, walked on water, healed the sick, cast out demons, and raised the dead. He taught with authority and gave the multitudes fresh revelation about the kingdom of God.

He also passed on this authority to His disciples. In fact, in the Bible, He never called anyone to minister without telling them to preach the gospel, cast out demons, and heal the sick. He commissioned His ministers and gave them government, authority and power.

Power in the Church

After demonstrating His power, Jesus sent out His disciples with authority and they taught and performed miracles as He did.

The apostles' anointing rose to a new level after His resurrection. When the Holy Spirit was given at Pentecost, the New Covenant church was birthed and the disciples were given governmental authority. They were commissioned to lead by example. They embraced godliness and ruled over the church with kindness, grace and authority.

The disciples became ambassadors of God's government. Whoever received the disciples received Jesus, and whoever rejected them rejected Him.

Jesus said, **"Whoever receives you receives me, and whoever receives me receives him who sent me." Mt. 10:40**

This is called the 'descending chain of authority'. In order to *have* authority a disciple must be *under* authority. All authority comes from God. He gave it to His Son, and through the Holy Spirit, that authority was given to His disciples.

Government in the Church

After Christ's resurrection, He ascended on high and did two things:

1. He filled the universe with Himself.
2. He gave gifts of government to men.

"He who descended is the very one who ascended higher than all the heavens, in order to fill the whole universe. <u>So Christ himself gave the apostles, the prophets, the evangelists, the pastors and teachers to equip his people for works of service, so that the body may be built up</u> until we all reach unity in the faith and in the knowledge of the Son of God and become mature, attaining to the measure of the fullness of Christ." Eph. 4:10-13 (Emphasis added)

We see that Christ gave some to be apostles, some to be evangelists, some to be prophets, and some to be pastors and teachers, for the building up of His church. These ministers are His senior government representatives. Even among these five main ministers there is a descending chain of government and authority.

We read: ***"And God has placed in the church <u>first of all apostles, second prophets, third teachers, then miracles,</u> then gifts of healing, of helping, of guidance, and of different kinds of tongues." 1 Cor. 12:28*** (Emphasis added)

Defining Government Offices

There are many good books written on the five-fold government offices. Therefore, I will not belabor their definitions, but only give a brief description. All of these ministries are given to teach and equip God's people for service until the church becomes mature and reaches the fullness of what we see in Christ.

Individually, none of us can be everything, but together in Christ we can do everything that is required. Teachers, evangelists, prophets, and apostles may travel and minister in other places, but the pastor must remain and minister at home most of the time. Here are some brief definitions:

<u>Teachers</u> are gifted with the authority and ability to explain the profound truths of Scripture in simple terms.

<u>Pastors</u> teach, lead, protect, and care for God's people, the sheep who are in the local church.

Evangelists preach to the unsaved and lead them to salvation. They also equip God's people to be witnesses of Christ.

Prophets who carry government function differently than those people who simply prophesy. Everyone may prophesy words that will strengthen, comfort and encourage. Prophets, however, also speak directional and governmental words over individuals, churches, and nations.

Apostles are in a different class of leadership. They are senior leaders under Christ. Without them the church can never reach maturity. Here are ten functions of a seasoned apostle:

1. Apostles are fathers. They make room for, and extend approbation over other ministers so that those ministers may function with confidence and authority in their appropriate office or ministry (1 Cor. 4:15).

2. Apostles are miracle workers. They carry supernatural power (2 Cor. 12:12).

3. Apostles are equippers. They mentor, train, equip, inspire, and help other ministers do the work of Christ that they are called to do (Eph. 4:11-12).

4. Apostles are motivators. They inspire the church to rise up and do great things (Acts 2:14-41).

5. Apostles are church planters. They travel to new territory and start new churches (Acts 16:11-40).

6. Apostles are pastors of pastors. They provide pastoral care and advice for pastors concerning their

personal lives and their ministry responsibilities (Phil. 4:9).

7. <u>Apostles are architects</u>. They help design and build churches so that they may function successfully in different communities, cultures and countries (1 Cor. 3:9-10).

8. <u>Apostles are troubleshooters</u>. They help churches and communities fix their practical and spiritual problems (1 Cor. 4:17-21).

9. <u>Apostles are networkers</u>. They cross denominational lines to bring different church groups together (Acts 11:1-18).

10. <u>Apostles establish sound doctrine</u>. They judge, define, affirm and communicate the teachings of the faith (Acts 15:6-35).

Today's Church

Most churches today are pastor/teacher led. They have little or no other five-fold ministers functioning among them. This produces a serious shortfall.

The primary task of pastors is maintenance. They feed, care for, and protect the sheep. Generally speaking, they do not bring increase or maturity. If a church, with just a pastor is growing in number, vision, or maturity it is likely because the pastor is also an evangelist, a teacher, a prophet, or an apostle.

Small churches are especially challenged with a lack of growth because it is unlikely that all of these five-fold government ministers will be present in their congregation. They must therefore invite ministers with these other gifts to come train, impart, and motivate their people with an increased level of God's government.

Without the impartation of these five offices, the practical government of God will be largely missing from the church, and the family of God will not develop according to God's master plan.

Many churches have no understanding of these ministries, and some refuse their input because of personal control issues or fear of their misuse.

Often, churches follow a democratic form for electing their pastors and running the church. This is not a Biblical pattern. While deacons, who administrate practical service, may be chosen by a democratic vote, five-fold ministers have authority from God, not people. Other five-fold ministers should ordain, appoint, confirm and hold their co-workers accountable. Their accountability should come from other five-fold ministers. They should not be under congregational government, control or direction. Senior ministers cannot lead with radical faith if they are subject to a congregation that is not gifted with government. The kingdom of God is a theocracy not a democracy.

A Time For God's Government

It is time for the government of God to emerge on a larger scale. Following this biblical mandate will be messy because of a lack of maturity, selfish ambition, and personal pride, but there is no other way. According to God's master plan, He gave these ministries for the building up of His church (see Eph. 4:11). That is plan A and He does not have plan B. The church cannot be built according to God's design without apostles, prophets, evangelists, pastors, and teachers taking their place. Let the ministers arise and let the church receive godly government and spiritual growth.

CHAPTER NINE

The Harvest

The Great Farmer

God's plan includes the 'harvest of the earth'. God is the great farmer. All farmers should follow His example. Farmers produce life, whether animals or vegetation. They bring seed to maturity and harvest a crop. They are methodical and patient, and in the end, they look for abundant increase.

Our Heavenly Father is the greatest farmer and He waits patiently for the harvest of the earth. He is looking for abundant increase. He is growing a huge family and in the end, He will produce a perfect world for His family to live in. It is more than just a revival of souls being saved; it is the maturing of a bride for His Son. The Bible emphasizes this harvest theme. The process comes to its fullness at the end of the age and is described in the book of Revelation.

We read: *"Then another angel came out of the temple and called in a loud voice to him who was sitting on the cloud, "Take your sickle and reap, because the time to reap has come, <u>for the harvest of the earth is ripe." so he who was seated on the cloud swung his sickle over the earth, and the earth was harvested</u>." Rev. 14:15-16* (Emphasis added)

The book of Revelation, with its great tribulation, is the hope of humanity. It tells us that at the end of the age, we will see the largest and greatest harvest in human history. The result is that vast multitudes enter the kingdom of God and become part of God's family. That is the primary purpose of the great tribulation.

Mercy Overpowers Judgment

The completion of the harvest comes as extensive tribulations and judgments are poured upon the earth. The hearts of multitudes are brought to tenderness under immense pressure, and out of great desperation people cry out to God and are saved.

This tribulation method for salvation was not God's first harvest approach. Throughout history He has beckoned with great patience, compassion, and kindness, but the response has not produced the fullness of the harvest. Mankind has continuously rebelled against God and often rejected His call.

The great tribulation is the judgment of the world and it is long overdue because of man's horrific sins. The sins have piled up so high that justice must finally come for the innocent and the defenseless. God, however, will use this season of pain. He will turn His judgment into an opportunity for redemption. The ultimate purpose of the great tribulation is the harvest of the earth.

The Lord of the Harvest

Jesus is called, "The Lord of the Harvest," and He looks for laborers to help Him bring the harvest in. He calls us to pray so that He may send workers into the world for this purpose (see Mt. 9:37-38).

There will be two great end-time harvests of the earth. One involves a revival in Israel and the other, a revival among the nations. Together, these revivals will produce the end-time, one new man Church. I believe that the redeemed of Israel and the Gentile church are the two witnesses that John was told about in Revelation eleven.

"'And I will give power to my two witnesses, and they will prophesy for 1,260 days, clothed in sackcloth.' These are the two olive trees and the two lampstands that stand before the Lord of the earth." Rev. 11:3-4 (see my book Unexpected Fire for more details)

In these verses, we discover that these two witnesses are olive trees and lampstands. In Scripture, the two olive trees and the lampstands represent redeemed Israel and the Gentile church (see Rom. 11 and Zech. I, 4, 6). We also discover that the lampstand in Revelation chapter one, verse twenty, represents the churches.

In the gospels, before the day of Pentecost, Jesus refers to the spiritual gathering of the Jewish people as the church (see Mt. 18:16, see also Acts 7:38). After Pentecost we see the church of the nations emerge. Revival will come to both Jews and Gentiles through Christ. (see my book Unexpected Fire for more details)

Revival in Israel

Concerning these two end-time revivals in Revelation, we are first introduced to the Jewish revival.

"Then I heard the number of those who were sealed: 144,000 from all the tribes of Israel." Rev. 7:4

A Jewish revival comes at the beginning of the great tribulation. The tribes of Israel are specifically mentioned in that revival and those saved are represented by a symbolic number of 144,000.

In the book Zechariah, we also read about the end-time, Jewish revival.

The Lord says, *"And I will pour out on the house of David and the inhabitants of Jerusalem a spirit of grace and of supplication. They will look on me, the one they have pierced, and they will mourn for him as one mourns for an only son." ... "On that day a fountain will be opened to the house of David and the inhabitants of Jerusalem, to cleanse them from sin and impurity." Zech. 12:10, 13:1*

The time period of this Jewish revival is also given in Zechariah twelve. The Jewish revival happens during a season when Israel is unmovable - a time when she receives supernatural military protection and supremacy from God. This can only refer to these last days. Only since 1948, and into the future, is Israel's unstoppable dynamic applicable. Before 1948, Israel never experienced this level of military strength. Read the entire chapter of Zechariah twelve and see it for yourself.

At that appointed time in the future, God's grace will bring the Jews to sorrow, supplication, and salvation. They will weep when they finally realize that Jesus is their Messiah. They will pray the prayers of repentance and supplication. Then millions of Jews will be saved (see Zech. 12:10,11 and Zech. 13:1-2)

Church Fathers Speak Up

Many church fathers preached about a Jewish revival at the end of the age. The following quotes are taken from the book, "The Puritan Hope; Revival and Interpretation of Prophecy," by Iain H. Murray.

Jonathan Edwards, a revivalist of the "Great Awakening in America", wrote, *"Nothing is more clearly foretold than this national conversion of the Jews in Romans eleven."*

Can you imagine what will happen to the Church around the world when multitudes of Israelites receive Jesus as their Messiah?

Romans eleven, verse fifteen says, ***"If the casting away of them be the reconciling of the world, what shall the receiving of them be but life from the dead."***

When revival comes to Israel, the Church will be invigorated to new life. The early Puritans believed this. They said, "The Scripture speaks of a double conversion of the Gentiles, the first before the conversion of the Jews, the second after the conversion of the Jews."

Thomas Boston of The Church of Scotland also preached this message. A sermon recorded from 1716 declares, *"Are you longing for a revival to the churches, then pray for the Jews. 'For if the casting away of them be the reconciling of the world; what shall the receiving of them be but life from the dead.' That will be a lively time, a time of great outpouring of the Spirit, that will carry reformation to a greater height than yet has been."*

In 1855, Charles Spurgeon preached the following, *"I think we do not attach sufficient importance to the restoration of the Jews. We do not think enough of it. But certainly, if there is anything promised in the Bible it is this. The day shall yet come when the Jews, who were the first apostles to the Gentiles, the first missionaries to us who were afar off, shall be gathered in again. Until that shall be, the fullness of the church's glory can never come. Matchless benefits to the world are bound up with the restoration of Israel; their gathering in shall be as life from the dead."*

Why Seven Years

The great tribulation is redemptive; it will bring international revival. That is why the judgments of the great tribulation last for seven full years. God could speak and the earth would be consumed, but He will not do that. Instead, He uses the seven years of the great tribulation to bring billions of people to repentance and salvation.

Many will still go to a hell, but hell fire was not primarily created for people. Hell was created for the devil and his angels. People go to hell because they are wicked, and because they persist in turning away from the Creator and His Christ.

World-Wide Revival

It is not just the Jews who will be saved at the end of time. Here is a picture of a worldwide harvest during the great tribulation.

"After this I looked and there before me was a great multitude that no one could count, <u>from every</u>

nation, tribe, people and language, standing before the throne and in front of the Lamb. They were wearing white robes and were holding palm branches in their hand ... Then one of the elders asked me, "These in white robes – who are they, and where did they come from?"... And he said, "<u>These are they who have come out of the great tribulation: they have washed their robes and made them white in the blood of the Lamb</u>." Rev. 7:9, 13-14 (Emphasis added)

Immediately following the Jewish revival, the Gentiles will experience a revival so large that (as the Scripture says) it will be impossible to count the number of souls that are saved. They will come from every nation and even from every subculture.

"If their [The Jewish People] *rejection is the reconciliation of the world, what will their acceptance be but life from the dead?" Rom. 11:15*

When revival comes to Israel, vast multitudes around the world will see it and come to Christ as well. As the aforementioned Scripture says, it will be like resurrection from the dead.

The One New Man is Prophesied

The great tribulation will activate the end-time church, and believers will rise to witness for Christ. Revival will erupt around the world as God's two historical witnesses, redeemed Jews and the Gentile church, partner together as one new man. The natural and the wild olive branches will function as one.

It is not the horrors of the great tribulation alone that will cause people to cry out to the Lord for mercy. It will also be the love, compassion, and service of the saints that will soften their hearts. Scripture says that the kindness of the Lord leads a man to repentance (see Rom. 2:4).

When people have nowhere to turn, many will discover the love of God flowing through the church. For ministers of the gospel, saving souls will become the most important thing during the great tribulation.

"Who are these people who make up this multitude and where have they come from?" Rev. 7:13

"These are they who have come out of the great tribulation; they have washed their robes and made them white in the blood of the Lamb." Rev. 7:14

Many Christians rightfully think of the great tribulation as a horrifying seven years, but most fail to observe the myriads of saved ones who will be promoted to heaven during that time. The Lord will receive His reward. It is called 'the latter rain', 'the end-time revival', 'the harvest of the earth'.

God Is Patient

Harvesting the earth was God's plan before He made the world. He has continually called people to the cross of Christ, and they have come from every nation. Throughout history, a steady harvest of souls have been saved, and only God knows who they are and how many have come. Still, God looks for a much greater harvest. He is patient, and at the end of the age, the great in-gathering of people on the planet will come to salvation in a brief season of time.

The Latter Rain

The end-time harvest is known in Scripture as 'the latter rain'. Here are a few verses that point to this reality:

*"<u>Therefore be patient, brethren, until the coming of the Lord. See how the farmer waits for the precious fruit of the earth, waiting patiently for it until it receives the early and latter rain</u>." **Js. 5:7 NKJV*** (Emphasis added)

"Be glad then you children of Zion, and rejoice in the Lord your God; for he has given you the former rain faithfully, and he will cause the rain to come down for you – The former rain, and the latter rain." Joel 2:23 NKJV

"Ask the Lord for rain in the time of the latter rain. The Lord will make flashing clouds; He will give them showers of rain, grass in the field for everyone." Zech. 10:1 NKJV

"Let us pursue the knowledge of the Lord. His going forth is established as the morning; He will

come to us like the rain, like the latter and the former rain to the earth." Hos. 6:3 NKJV

"Then I will give you the rain for your land in its season, the early rain and the latter rain, that you may gather in your grain, your new wine and your oil." Deut. 11:14 NKJV

At the halfway point of the great tribulation, massive revivals come. It happens so quickly that it is compared to the single stroke of a farmer's sickle. Millions of evangelists will share the testimony of Christ among the nations. The result will be the greatest harvest of souls in history.

International Revival

Jesus said, *"And this gospel of the kingdom will be preached in all the world as a testimony to all nations and then the end shall come." Mt. 24:14*

Preachers will become numerous. The global harvest is the ultimate reason for the cross. The Church, along with redeemed, Messianic Israel, will rise to the challenge of being Christ's witnesses. Understanding the end-time harvest allows multitudes of believers to volunteer freely and go forward, into the future, with excitement.

The gospel of the kingdom will be preached in all the world <u>and then the end shall come</u>. Christians will become bold in their faith and the amazing witness of Christ and His kingdom will be phenomenal.

The work of believers will be in partnership with a host of angels. Together, people and angels will serve the Lord of Glory.

"Then I saw another angel flying in midair, and <u>he had the eternal gospel to proclaim</u> to those who live on the earth - to every nation, tribe, language and people." Rev. 14:6 (Emphasis added)

I believe that gangs, criminals, the disadvantaged, and displaced persons will be among the first to come to the Lord. Ethnic minorities, people from ghettoes, the homeless, and the violent will experience reformation. From hopelessness, they will rise to joy and salvation, and the earth will be harvested.

Many wealthy and influential leaders will also come to Christ, but only as they let go of their pride and put their trust in the Living God. The Bible tells us that it is hard for a rich man to enter the kingdom, but in due season, they will come as well. This is God's plan.

"The harvest <u>is the end of the age</u> and the harvesters are angels." Mt. 13:39 (Emphasis added)

People and angels will work together and the Lord will save every weary and hungry soul who calls out to Him. The harvest is His reward.

CHAPTER TEN

Called Into Fellowship

The Only Thing That Counts

We have already studied the journey of man, but it is fitting for us to talk about the journey of the disciple. After all, God is looking for teachable disciples. He is preparing a fabulous family, a bride without spot or wrinkle for His Son.

We know that we have been called out of the ungodly system of this world, but what have we been called into? The answer is given to us in the Bible.

*"**God is faithful, who has called you <u>into fellowship</u> with his Son, Jesus Christ our Lord." 1 Cor. 1:9*** (Emphasis added)

> *"We proclaim to you what we have seen and heard, so that you also may have fellowship with us. And our fellowship is with the Father and with his Son, Jesus Christ." 1 Jn.1:3*

We are called into fellowship with one another and with the Lord. The journey that God has planned for us is summed up in a single verse: ***"The only thing that counts is faith expressing itself in love." Gal. 5:6*** (Emphasis added)

That is the essence of fellowship. Once we commit our lives under the government of God and accept Jesus as Savior, an epic quest opens before us. It is the upward call to gain the prize, which is our full inheritance in Christ. Eventually, we will become heirs of all things, but we are called to travel a transforming journey of love before our inheritance can be complete.

To gain the fullness of our inheritance, there are two paths that cannot be circumnavigated. We must love God and love people. These paths are interwoven and one cannot be travelled without the other. The ultimate plan that God has for us is fellowship. That fellowship is relational. It is all about love.

Two Kinds of People

There are two kinds of people on the earth: relaters and achievers, but God says relaters have found the most important of the two, because to relate effectively is to love. Children are natural relaters, many women are also relaters, but men often find this to be a difficult task.

"Now these three remain: faith, hope and love. But the greatest of these is love." 1 Cor. 13:13

After all is said and done, faith working with love is the only thing that counts. Faith is absolute trust in another, so much so that you are willing to commit without constraint. This only works effectively if you love someone.

Love is a flow of overwhelming admiration and passion that allows one person to give of themselves to another. It grows when there is an extraordinary trust in the relationship. If faith breaks down in a marriage it means that love is lost. The opposite is also true, if love is lost there will be a breakdown of faith and trust.

Marriage Love

If love or trust is damaged, it takes a long time, lots of patience, and excessive hard work to find them again.

"Husbands love your wives, just as Christ loved the church and gave himself up for her to make her holy... In this same way, husbands ought to love their wives as their own bodies." Eph. 5:25-28

The Lord gave us marriage; it is a building block in the plans of God. Our relationship with Jesus is compared to marriage.

God Invented Marriage

God has given us three institutions - civil government, the church, and marriage. Each of these is designed to help us live and work together.

God invented marriage to teach us how to walk in love and faith in the most intimate of ways. When marriage works it is magnificent. A successful marriage requires humility, sacrifice, intimacy, and service, but all the blessings make these sacrifices worthwhile. To share the fullness of life with another person in marriage is a taste of heaven on earth. It is the height of godly fellowship because it allows complete discovery, and in the process, one's joy can be complete.

People who do not know love have a huge hole inside of them. God made us for love and that love will be fully realized in the future world He will create. God is love and love between Jesus, the Father, and His family, is the end goal of His plan. It is the only thing that counts.

Intimacy

In marriage a sexual bond is made but there is more to intimacy than sex. Intimacy is sharing the deepest treasures of our hearts with someone. We call this vulnerability.

It is scary to be vulnerable with someone you do not trust, because you could be betrayed and hurt; but vulnerability with someone you trust is amazing.

Learning Love

My wife, Joy, and I were eighteen and twenty-one respectively, when we were married. She was beautiful and we were deeply in love. We had dated for three years before we tied the knot. But suddenly, after our vows, we were living together, and we faced new challenges.

After the honeymoon and three months had passed, it seemed like we had talked about everything possible. Things started to get quiet between us, and I felt we were slowly slipping apart. I remember talking with the Lord about it. I said to Him that I would always be faithful and loving toward my wife even though I felt like something was missing. I prayed and asked God to strengthen our friendship and help our relationship remain intimate and special.

Soon after that, we experienced some terrible attacks against our character and ministry. At twenty-one, I was already a pastor and I was facing unrelenting criticism from an older leader in the church. He was young in the Lord, just newly saved, and we were a small church. Even though he was just saved we elevated him to be one of the department leaders in the church. The Scriptures warn against doing this with a new believer because they could be puffed up with pride and cause trouble. That is exactly what happened, and Joy and I were at the other end of his slanderous attacks.

Eventually, God worked it out, but not before Joy and I lived in a lot of pain for many months. People in the church would come to us crying as they told us the evil things that this man was saying to them. We found ourselves putting out fires every day for weeks on end.

I remember sharing with Joy the excruciating pain and slander I was experiencing and I listened as she told me of her hurts and traumas as well. It was an awful time, but then one day, as she was preparing a meal in the kitchen and I was watching her from the other room, I thought, "I really love that lady."

Immediately, I remembered my conversation with the Lord and how I had asked Him to help us keep our relationship intimate and special. I asked myself what happened to shift us back. I concluded it was our vulnerability with each other that had made the difference. As we opened up and shared our deep pains with each other, God united our hearts in love and appreciation for each other once again.

Intimacy Again

When we are intimate, we share our likes and dislikes, our hopes and dreams, our strengths and weaknesses, and our pains and sorrows. We synergize with each other, make adjustments, and agree where we can until we are unified. We support, serve, and encourage each another, and if it goes both ways, we will feel cared for, and inspired to press forward and achieve.

Sex is reserved for marriage, but the intimacy I am speaking of is the fellowship of the church family, and a very personal relationship with the Living God. These levels of fellowship require the opening of our hearts. We must learn a special level of communication, one that is overflowing with the fruit of the Spirit. This type of sharing is filled with joy, goodness, kindness, gentleness, peace, patience, faithfulness, self-control, and, of course, love. The communication of life given with these qualities produces real fellowship. We have been called out of the mindset of the world, and into the fellowship of God's dear Son (see 1 Cor. 1:9). That is His plan.

Godliness or Garbage

Before leaving this chapter, we need to look at the nature of our love and discover what godly unity consists of. Fellowship is sharing things we have in common and it is essential to the plan of God. The wicked or ungodly, however, can come into unity just like good people can. They can have an affinity and camaraderie, and even an intimacy that is caring, deep and committed. They can enjoy one another in their evil

Understanding God's Great Plan

pursuits, but in the end, the wages of sin is always death. Everything in a garbage bin can be unified and compacted into one solid cube, but it is still garbage.

God's plan is not just unity and vulnerability, it is also goodness. The tower of Babel is an example of unity for the wrong reasons. That is why the sanctifying process of transformation is part of God's plan as well. He does not just want us to feel good, He wants us to be good.

The kingdom of God is righteousness, peace, and joy in the Holy Spirit (see Rom. 14:17). If we do not have righteousness, we will not have peace and joy. Before the end comes, those who are holy will become more holy and those who are unholy will become even more unholy (see Rev. 22:11).

We are called to be holy as God is holy, and by His power and grace we will be. Then we will fellowship in a world full of love. Why would God want a new world if it is not different from the old one? The Lord will make all things new. He calls us to love one another as He has loved us.

He says, *"A new commandment I give you: Love each other. Just as I have loved you, you should love one another." Jn. 13:34*

It is no longer good enough for us to just love our neighbor as we love ourselves. After all, some people do not have a great love for themselves. If, however, we love others as Christ has loved us, there will be nothing lacking in our love. Our fellowship will be complete.

PART THREE

A Kingdom Without End

CHAPTER ELEVEN

Myriads of Angels

Angels in Antiquity

Long before we existed, God created angels. They were with Him when He laid the foundations of the earth.

"Where were you when I laid the earth's foundation?... while the morning stars sang together and all the angels shouted for joy?" Job 38:4,7

When anyone comes to Christ, they come to a lot more than they realize; they come to an amazing kingdom filled with wonders. The book of Hebrews gives us an indication of what God's kingdom consists of, and among its many attributes are myriads of angels, gathered in joyful assembly.

You get more than you asked for when you come to Jesus. You arrive to find multitudes of angels that are already there, gathered in God's presence. There are so many of them that they are innumerable. There are billions of them.

"But you have come to Mount Zion, to the city of the living God, the heavenly Jerusalem. You have come to thousands upon thousands [myriads NAS] [innumerable company KJV] *of angels in joyful assembly." Heb. 12:22*

Celestial Servants

God designed angels as part of His master plan. They were created for worship, warfare and works of service. They have a free will and, along with Satan, some of them rebelled against their creator and became fallen angels. This was such an extraordinary act of treason that God created hell fire to deal with their outrageous wickedness and pride.

Even fallen angels are forced to serve God's master plan. He uses them and demons to test humanity but they are restrained to limited abilities and measured activities of evil. God uses angels, both good and bad, as examples of what people should and should not do. He uses the fallen ones to tempt humanity so that mankind can choose between good or evil. Without that temptation people would have no choices. The fallen angels and demons have a limited time of freedom for they will not be around when Christ's thousand-year reign on earth begins.

"For if God did not spare angels when they sinned, but sent them to hell, putting them in chains of darkness to be held for judgment;... if this is so, then the Lord knows how to rescue the godly from trials and to hold the unrighteous for punishment on the day of judgment." 2 Pet. 2:4,9

Good angels embody dignity and joyfulness. They are servants of the Most High God and they partner with Him to accomplish His master plan. Here is an angel talking with John about Christ's coming kingdom and testimony.

"Then the angel said to me, 'Write this: Blessed are those who are invited to the wedding supper of the Lamb!'... I am your fellow servant with you and your brothers and sisters who hold to the testimony of Jesus." Rev. 19:9,10

Angels were with God before the world was created, and we know they worshipped and served Him in eternity past (see Ezek. 28:13-18). We do not know many details, however, of their life and purpose before Adam and Eve arrived in the Garden of Eden. It seems that once the earth was formed, God turned the attention of angels to the care, purpose and service of the human race.

Angels Serve God's People

Almost all of the heroes of the Bible had amazing encounters with angels. We discover stories of angels from the first book of the Bible to the last. They not only serve God, but have been commissioned to serve His people as well.

"Are not all angels ministering spirits sent to serve those who will inherit salvation?" Heb. 1:14

Their service begins with newborn babies. Every child has been created in the image of God and each is fearfully and wonderfully made. Each child has been assigned an angel and when that child or a parent of that child, calls out to God, the angel is there to serve and fight on behalf of that little one.

"See that you do not despise one of these little ones. For I tell you that their angels in heaven always see the face of my Father in heaven." Mt. 18:10

Not all battles over the lives of children are won, and at some point, an angel may be released from their care of a child. This is a sad story but it is because of sin, and not necessarily the sin of the child. All removal of God's resources and all of the corruption that is in the world is a result of sin (see 2 Pet. 1:4).

Besides serving and protecting children, angels serve believers and disciples in five different ways.

1. They protect - Ps 34:7
2. They bring provisions - 1 Kgs. 19:5
3. They bring direction - Acts 10:3
4. They bring comfort - Mt. 4:11, Lk. 22:43
5. They help a person fulfill their God-given destiny - Acts 8:26, Acts 23:11

Undercover Government Agents

Angels are undercover agents who worship before God's throne and serve His eternal purpose. They were created with diverse looks, skills and purpose, but all of them are powerful.

Like soldiers of a vast army, they live under a chain of command with levels of authority and positions of lesser or greater roles of government. Some are called princes and archangels, others are seraphim and cherubim. They have charge over massive companies of soldier angels and some of them are commissioned to protect nations and people groups on the earth (see Dan. 10:21, 12:1). They have thrones, dominions, principalities, powers, and authorities. Each of these terms describes a specific level of angelic government.

As mentioned earlier in the book, some animals on earth were blessed when created because they were made to look like some of these angels. Some angels have faces of lions, eagles, oxen and some look like horses (see Ezek. 1:10, Zech. 6:1-8).

"The first chariot had red horses, the second black, the third white, and the fourth dappled - all of them powerful. I asked the angel who was speaking to me, "What are these, my lord?" The angel answered me, "These are the four spirits of heaven, going out from standing in the presence of the Lord of the whole world." Zech. 6:2-5

Note that the angels were there before animals were created on earth, so some earth creatures have been made in their likeness, and not the other way around. Some angels have wings like huge storks and others have as many as six wings (see Zech. 5:9, Isa. 6:2). Some have hundreds of eyes all over their bodies. There is no sneaking up on them; they will always see you coming. In warfare the cherubim and seraphim are unbeatable.

They can fly, travel through walls, and move through space. They can suddenly appear in the sky, or in your house, or in your dreams. If the occasion calls for it, they can appear as men or women, or bright blinding lights.

They can move together in absolute unity like a flock of birds or a massive school of fish darting to the left or right in synchronized choreography (see Ezek. 1:1-48). They are wheels within wheels, covered in eyes and millions of them can move together as a single being, as the Spirit of God leads them.

End Time Angels

Angels are not just a Bible phenomena; at least a third of the congregation of our local church say they have seen an angel. Documented testimonies of their protective activity during warfare are numerous. The first and second world wars and many wars since, have left us with stories from soldiers who tell of protection and salvation because of angels.

Untold thousands of testimonies from common people, in everyday situations, continue to reveal encounters with angels.

The books of the Bible that focus on end of time prophecy, promise us that increased angel encounters are before us (see Zech. 12:7-9 and the entire book of Revelation). These futuristic appearances of angels bring protection to God's people but also judgment to the wicked, just like the death angel did in Egypt during the time of the exodus. More angels will be coming at the end of the age.

"The harvest is the end of the age and the harvesters are the angels." Mt. 13:39

They will come, en mass, from heaven when Jesus returns. All the armies of heaven will descend with the Lord, at His second coming (see Rev. 19:11,14). Most of the armies that are coming will be angels.

The Bible does not tell us what angels will be doing during Christ's millennial reign on earth but they will be there with us. We will be in God's presence and in the presence of the holy angels. One thing is for sure; angels will always play an amazing role in God's master plan. I know that angels and people will forever be co-partners with Christ. I wonder if we will be personal friends.

CHAPTER TWELVE

The Second Coming

Revelation

The book of Revelation is the completion of the cross. Everything that Jesus died for on the cross is finalized in the Apocalypse. All the promises that God presents to us in the Bible are fulfilled at the end of time.

The scroll is opened, the judgments come, and God's mercy is extended to all who will receive. By the time the seven years of the great tribulation are over, the world will be devastated, the massive harvest will be brought in, and Jesus will return to the earth to set up His millennial kingdom.

The return of Christ, which we call the second coming, has a monumental purpose. When He comes with His holy angels, Jesus puts everything in order; He resurrects His family, destroys evil and begins the process of earth's restoration. He then completes the master plan of God for this age.

The Second Coming

At the end of the book of Revelation, in the nineteenth chapter, we read about the return of the Lord.

It says, *"I saw heaven standing open and there before me was a white horse, whose rider is called faithful and true. With justice he judges and wages war." Rev. 19:11*

Jesus descends from heaven and the righteous who are dead come back to life. Then, we who are alive and remain until His coming, shall be caught up into the clouds and be changed in a twinkling of an eye. Then we shall forever be with the Lord.

"Listen, I tell you a mystery: We shall not all sleep, but we will all be changed - in a flash, in a twinkling of an eye, at the last trumpet. For the trumpet will sound, the dead shall be raised imperishable, and we shall be changed. For the perishable must clothe itself with the imperishable, and the mortal with immortality." 1 Cor. 15:51-53

The second coming of Christ is what all believers look for. It is resurrection day.

The Second Coming

"For the Lord himself will come down from heaven, with a loud command, with the voice of the archangel and with the trumpet call of God, and the dead in Christ will rise first. After that, we who are still alive and are left will be caught up together with them in the clouds to meet the Lord in the air. And so we shall ever be with the Lord." 1 Thes. 4:16-17

The Bible says that when Jesus appears we will be like Him. This seems unthinkable, yet since becoming God's children, believers receive a new spirit and are born again. Then the sanctifying process begins, and we receive a huge transformation of soul, character, and perspective. When Jesus comes, however, the change will be much more dynamic. At that time we receive a new body, and the flaws that still remain in our understanding and character will be eradicated. We will be like Jesus.

Scripture says, *"Dear friends, now we are the children of God, and what we will be has not yet been known. But we know that when Christ appears, <u>we shall be like him, for we shall see him as he is</u>." 1 Jn. 3:2* (Emphasis added)

Just Like Jesus

What does it mean when the Bible says we shall be like Him? Revelation gives us a hint of what Jesus looks like today. We should understand that His appearance has changed since He went to heaven.

Following His resurrection and ascension, John, the revelator, saw Him in a vision. In my opinion, that is most likely what He looks like today. In John's vision, Jesus was so dynamic that when John saw Him, he thought he was going to die.

"I saw seven golden lampstands, and among the lampstands was someone like a son of man, dressed in a robe reaching down to his feet and with a golden sash around his chest. His head and hair were white like wool, as white as snow, and his eyes were like blazing fire. His feet were like bronze glowing in a furnace, and his voice was like the sound of rushing waters. In his right hand he held seven stars, and out of his mouth came a sharp double edged sword. His face was like the sun shining in all its brilliance. When I saw him I fell at his feet as though dead." Rev. 1:12-17

Once again, at the end of the book of Revelation, we see a description of Jesus as well. It is the time of the second coming.

"His eyes are like blazing fire, and on his head are many crowns... He is dressed in a robe dipped in blood... Out of his mouth comes a sharp sword... On his robe and on His thigh he has this name written: KING OF KINGS AND LORD OF LORDS." Rev. 11:12, 13, 15, 16

When Jesus comes again, He is no longer the gentle rabbi from Galilee; He is the warrior king of heaven. Jesus appears as a blaze of unstoppable fire. When I read the verse that says we will be like Him, it causes me to wonder, in what ways we will be like Him.

What is Jesus Like?

Here is a short list of what we know about who Jesus is. Let's be clear, there is no limit to His character, governance, and glory. We cannot describe all of that, but we can mention a few details that describe His being, relative to His human family.

Jesus is, eternal, immortal, incorruptible, all knowing, all present, all-powerful, all loving, and He is supernatural in every way. That means He is not subject to the natural laws of physics. He is not natural; He is supernatural. He lives in a reality that denies the limitations of natural laws. He lives in the world of miracles.

What Will We Be Like?

The Bible gives specifics of what the future holds for those who love the Lord. God's master plan is to bless His Son with a great family and that is why, at the second coming, our upgrade will be so magnificent.

It takes a faith from heaven to believe God's promise of what we will become. The Bible says we will be like Him. In general terms, we know that to be true, but Scripture also gives us amazing details of the specifics that are in store for us.

1. We will be immortal (never dying) - 1 Cor. 15:53
2. We will be incorruptible - 1 Cor. 15:53
3. We will know fully, even as we are known - 1 Cor. 13:12
4. We will have a perfect spirit - Heb. 12:23
5. We will have a supernatural body, like Christ's - Phil. 3:21
6. We will have the Lord's name on our foreheads - Rev. 22:4
7. We will be in the service of the Lord - Rev. 22:3
8. Jesus can fly - I imagine we will as well - Acts 1:9
9. Jesus was translated from place to place - I imagine we will be - Mt. 28:16-17
10. Jesus walked through walls - I imagine we will as well - Jn. 20:26
11. We will have authority to rule - 2 Tim. 2:12
12. We can travel the cosmos, between planets - Rev. 19:14

God's plan for us, goes beyond what anyone has heard or seen (see 1 Cor. 2:9). The resurrection mentioned in the Bible takes place when our spirits are reunited with our bodies. Then everything about us will be perfected according to God's original plan. The Bible calls it the redemption of the body and the manifestation of the children of God.

"We ourselves, who have the firstfruits of the Spirit, groan inwardly as we wait eagerly for our

adoption to sonship, the redemption of our bodies." Rom. 8:23

The transformation in God's plan begins with people, but then it extends to the animals and to the entire planet.

"For the creation waits in eager expectation for the children of God to be revealed... The creation itself will be liberated from its bondage to decay and brought into the freedom and glory of the children of God." Rom. 8:19, 21

All of the animals and all of creation wait for the manifestation of the sons of God. When God's people are raised to newness of life, something is triggered in the world. The whole of creation is raised to supernatural life as well. The world will experience renewal and we will reign with Christ. In the next chapter we will see what the Bible says about this amazing new world and our purpose in it.

CHAPTER THIRTEEN

The Millennial Kingdom

A Thousand Years

God's plans will one day include a radical overhaul of the planet. Millennium means 'one thousand'. The thousand-year period when Christ reigns on earth is mentioned six times in the book of Revelation. It begins after the great tribulation and ends when Jesus presents the kingdom back to God the Father.

"Then the end will come, when he hands over the kingdom to God the Father after he has destroyed all dominion, authority and power." 1 Cor. 15:24

Handing the kingdom back to the Father happens at the end of Christ's thousand-year reign. First, however, Jesus spends a millennium with His family.

Many who are born during this time also have opportunity to submit under His rule. At the end of the thousand years He will destroy every other authority, dominion, and power, just as 1 Corinthians 15:24 says.

In these next two chapters we will focus on the new millennium. Prophetic words that are given to us personally are God's opportunities for us. They usually have conditions attached to them, and when people do not meet God's conditions the prophecies are not fulfilled. Most people who go to heaven do so without seeing the full completion of their personal prophecies.

Prophecies mentioned in the Bible, that point to God's eternal plan, are very different than personal prophecies. They always happen as designed, and they are not conditional or negotiable. They cannot be altered by the activities of man. The millennium is one of those unalterable prophecies.

Christ's Rule

Here is a picture of Christ's rule over the nations during the millennium.

"In the last days the mountain of the LORD'S temple will be established as the highest of the mountains; it will be exalted above the hills, and all nations will stream to it. Many peoples will come and say, 'Come, let us go up to the mountain of the LORD, to

The Millennial Kingdom

the temple of the God of Jacob. He will teach us his ways, so that we may walk in his paths.' The law will go out from Zion, the word of the LORD from Jerusalem. He will judge between nations and will settle disputes for many peoples. They will beat their swords into plowshares and their spears into pruning hooks. Nation will not take up sword against nation, nor will they train for war anymore." Isa. 2:2-4

From the nations of the saved, multitudes of people will stream to Jerusalem to be with the Lord. The rule of planet earth was once given to Adam and Eve to manage, and they failed. In the millennium, under the rule of King Jesus, it will be amazing; He will not fail.

He will rule with a rod of iron. It will be a compassionate rule, but with a strong hand. The Lord will not do this singlehandedly but will assign nations and cities to be ruled by those people who have served Him with distinction (see Lk. 19:17, Ps. 2, Ps. 110:2, Isa.11:4, Isa.61:2, Rev. 2:27, Rev. 12:5). The Lord works with a reward system so that those who serve with distinction in this life, are promoted with honors in the next.

The coming kingdom will be a world with a King and His people living in righteousness, peace and joy. There will be no wars for a thousand years. Weapons previously used in war, will be refashioned as agricultural implements to be used on amazing, superproductive farms around the world.

The Feasts

Some people call them the Jewish feasts, but the Bible calls them the feasts of the Lord (see Lev. 23). Passover, Unleavened Bread, First Fruits, Pentecost, Trumpets, Day of Atonement, and Tabernacles are the seven feasts of the Lord (I have used their Christian-Bible names so that many can identify them, but they have different names in Hebrew). They are Pesach, Hag Hamazot, Bikkurim, Shavuot, Rosh Hashanah, Yom Kippur, and Sukkot. The Sabbath day of rest is also a special feast of the Lord mentioned in this list. It is celebrated weekly.

Each feast is fulfilled in Christ.

1. They had a special meaning for the Jewish people under the Old Covenant.
2. They have a more complete meaning under the New Covenant.
3. We will understand their full meaning and purpose in the millennium.

I believe that every nation, whether Jewish or Gentile, will send representatives to Jerusalem to celebrate the feasts. The Lord will insist on it. The Feast of Tabernacles is mentioned and the Gentile nations will definitely come to celebrate that feast.

"Then the survivors from all the nations that have attacked Jerusalem will go up year after year to

worship the King, the LORD Almighty, and to celebrate the Festival of Tabernacles. If any of the peoples of the earth do not go up to Jerusalem to worship the King, the LORD Almighty, they will have no rain. If the Egyptian people do not go up and take part, they will have no rain. The LORD will bring on them the plague he inflicts on the nations that do not go up to celebrate the Festival of Tabernacles." Zech. 14:16-18

Even though we will be living in a new and glorious world, the Lord insists that we celebrate the journey of God and His people. He insists that we worship the One who brought us here. I believe that the Feast of Tabernacles is designed to help us keep that focus.

Cultural Changes

A celebration of the feasts is not the only cultural change that Gentiles will experience. Get ready for many things to change. For example, the days of the week will no longer be called Monday, Tuesday, Wednesday and so on. The months of the year will no longer be called January, February, etc. The days and months are all named after the demon gods of ancient Greek and Roman cultures. Pagan ideology and false gods will not tolerated in the millennium.

Even Easter is named after a Roman goddess. In our present world, Easter celebrates the death, burial, and resurrection of Christ, but Easter, as we know it, was once called Passover, Unleavened Bread, and First Fruits.

The days of the week, the months of the year, and the celebration of Christ's death, burial, and resurrection are great, but the names we have assigned them did not come from God. Those names are not good and will not remain. Get ready for the world to go back to using the original Jewish names for the days of the week, months, and feasts. They have names given by the Lord.

Before the Lord returns, it is not likely that we will change these things, but in the millennium all things will be made new.

A New Heaven and Earth

Before righteousness, peace, and joy can fully return, the earth will undergo a massive restoration. By the end of the great tribulation, the earth, sea, and sky will be so decimated by the judgments of God that the world will be uninhabitable (see my book Unexpected Fire). The ozone layer will be depleted, all life in the oceans will die, and the vegetation on earth will be burned up. All fresh water on the surface of the planet will become poisonous and the earth will be demolished by earthquakes, flaming asteroids and hundred pound hail stones. We will need a new earth and a new heaven (a new atmosphere).

> *"See, I will create new heavens and a new earth. The former things will not be remembered, nor will they come to mind." Isa. 65:17*
>
> *"Then I saw "a new heaven and a new earth," for the first heaven and the first earth had passed away." Rev. 21:1*

According to God's plan, the great tribulation is de-evolution. In other words, everything falls apart. It is followed, however, by the restoration of all things. At the second coming, Jesus returns to earth and the time of eternal refreshing and restoration will start.

> *"Repent, then, and turn to God, so that your sins may be wiped out, that times of refreshing may come from the Lord, and that he may send the Messiah, who has been appointed for you - even Jesus. Heaven must receive him until the time comes for God to restore everything, as he promised long ago through his holy prophets." Acts 3:19*

People Help

The earth, sea, and the atmosphere of the planet will be supernaturally restored by the Lord Himself. The ozone layer will be instantly replenished and earthquake chasms in the earth's surface will be fused together. Seas and fresh water will be restored to purity and life. All of that will happen miraculously by the Creator who made them in the first place.

People will also help with the clean up. For more than seven months after Christ's return, His sons and daughters will be burying the bodies of the multitudes that have died during the great tribulation. Then, for seven years, people will be burning the weapons, used in the end-time battles, as fuel.

"People will be continually employed in cleansing the land. They will spread out across the land and, along with others, they will bury any bodies that are lying on the ground. After the seven months they will carry out a more detailed search. As they go through the land, anyone who sees a human bone will leave a marker beside it until the gravediggers bury it... And so they will cleanse the land." Ezek.39:14-16

"Then those who live in the towns of Israel will go out and use the weapons as fuel and burn them up... For seven years they will use them for fuel." Ezek. 39:9

The Marriage Supper of the Lamb

I believe the new millennium can also be called 'the marriage supper of Lamb' (see Rev. 19:7-9, Mt. 22:1-14, Mt. 25:1-13). This is a thousand year extended celebration of God's Son and His bride (the Church).

The marriage begins at the end of the book of Revelation. We read about it in Revelation chapter nineteen, the same chapter that tells us about the return of Christ. As we discover, the marriage supper of the

The Millennial Kingdom

Lamb does not happen at the beginning of the great tribulation. The marriage feast celebration, lasts for one thousand years. The planet will be like a new Garden of Eden, only this time, it will be led by a new couple, Christ and His church. He is called the last Adam.

"So it is written, 'The first Adam became a living being;' the last Adam, a life-giving spirit... The first man was of the dust of the earth, the second man is of heaven." 1 Cor. 15:45,47

"They will say, 'This desolate land has become like <u>the garden of Eden</u>, and the waste, desolate, and ruined cities are fortified and inhabited.'" Ezek. 36:35 (Emphasis added)

"The LORD will surely comfort Zion and will look with compassion on all her ruins; he will make her deserts like <u>Eden</u>, her wastelands like the garden of the LORD. Joy and gladness will be found in her, thanksgiving and the sound of singing." Isa. 51:3 (Emphasis added)

CHAPTER FOURTEEN

Life in the Millennium

Two Kinds of People

We have been studying the thousand-year reign of Christ on earth that begins right after His second coming. According to God's eternal plan, the Bible teaches that two kinds of people will be in the new millennium, mortals and immortals. People who are Christ's at His coming will become like Him; they will be immortal and incorruptible. Other people, however, will not be immortal. We know this because, when the millennium is over, and Satan is released to tempt the nations, many follow him and are killed. People cannot die if they are immortal, so mortals are also on earth during the millennium (see Rev. 20).

Mortals

Where do the mortals come from? Who are they, and why are they in Christ's new kingdom? Some are survivors of those who attacked Jerusalem (see Zech. 14:16). Perhaps they did not have opportunity for salvation, and God does not destroy people unjustly.

Some of the mortals in the new millennium are faith-filled Jews who will be in Jerusalem when Christ returns. Before the return of Christ, they will not believe that Jesus is the Messiah, and therefore, they do not receive new bodies and immortality when He comes. They have faith in the God of Abraham, however, and will be looking for the Messiah. It is unfortunate that they will still be living at the level of their Old Covenant revelation when Christ returns.

The battle of Armageddon will be raging at the end of the age, and many Jews in Jerusalem will be under attack (see Zech. 14:1-4). Suddenly, the eastern sky will open and the Lord Himself will descend, with the armies of heaven, to resurrect those who have believed in Him. It will happen in a twinkling of an eye.

Then, in an instant, following the resurrection, Jesus Christ will descend to the Mount of Olives to destroy sinners, and deal with the devil, his demons, and the fallen angels.

At that moment, many Jews who previously did not receive Jesus as Messiah, will suddenly believe in

Him. It will be an incredible 'wow,' moment. These Jews already believe in the Living God, but then they will also believe that Jesus is the Christ. They will begin to worship Him, and Christ will rescue them from the sinners who are attacking (see Zech. 14:4-9).

They will not be sent to hell because they have now met God's requirements for salvation, but they will not yet become immortal; they were not Christ's at His coming. Although late in the game, so to speak, they have believed in the Lord Jesus Christ and will therefore be saved.

Many Babies Born

Other mortals will arrive after the millennium begins. They are children. Once the mortals enter the new millennium, they will marry and have many children. Scripture tells us that there will be no miscarriages, and people will live to be one thousand years old during the millennium. Even if someone dies at one hundred years old, they will be considered a youth, and it will be said that they died because they sinned and were cursed.

"Never again will there be an infant who lives but a few days, or an old man who does not live out his years; the one who dies at one hundred will be thought a mere child; the one who fails to reach a hundred will be considered accursed." Isa. 65:20

Because of long life, amazing health, and abundant productivity, many billions of babies will be born during the millennium. Ultimately, the Lord wants a huge family in His new kingdom.

There will be no demons, very little sickness, and very few deaths, so the earth will become populated beyond our imagination. The planet will not be overcrowded however, because it will be managed with excellence. There will be plenty of food, plenty of room, and new job opportunities here on earth when things are done right.

Animals and Vegetarians

With the exception of eating fish, everyone on the planet will be a vegetarian. The lion will lie with the lamb and the wolf will eat straw like the ox. There will be no killing or hurt in all of God's new world (see Isa. 11).

The Dead Sea will teem with all kinds of fish, and fishermen will be there mending their nets, so I expect we will be eating fish (see Ezek. 47:10).

The Jews put fish in a separate category from other meat because it does not have the breath of life in it. In the time of Noah's great flood, those creatures who had the breath of life were killed, but fish were spared.

There will be lots of children in the millennium and Scripture speaks of them. Infant children will play with poisonous snakes, and will lead huge mammals around as well (see Isa. 11). Can you imagine having a polar bear or a tiger as a pet? It might be expensive to feed them (veggies only), but it would be so much fun.

"The wolf will live with the lamb, the leopard will lie down with the goat, the calf and the lion and the yearling together; and a little child will lead them. The cow will feed with the bear, their young will lie down together, and the lion will eat straw like the ox. The infant will play near the cobra's den, and the young child will put his hand into the viper's nest. They will neither harm nor destroy on all my holy mountain, for the earth will be filled with the knowledge of the LORD as the waters cover the sea." Isa. 11:6-9

Healing for the Nations

Although immortals are incorruptible, the mortals will need medical assistance to help them live for a thousand years, and Jesus will provide it. From under His throne in Jerusalem, supernatural water will flow like a river, down to the Dead Sea. It will bring the sea back to life and it will teem with all kinds of fish. Wherever the river water goes, life will follow.

The tree of life will be in Jerusalem, and on both sides of the river all kinds of trees will grow. Their fruit and leaves will contain miraculous power. Each tree will bear twelve different fruit, and their leaves will be for the healing of the nations.

Family Decisions

I can imagine the words of the young mother whose husband is leaving their home in New York City to visit the temple mount during the Feast of Tabernacles.

She lines up all twenty-two of her young children instructing them to kiss their dad before he leaves. Then she says, **"Judah, please make sure you bring a fresh bag of temple leaves and a thermos of the water of life when you return. And remember to pray for extra blessings over our land and family, especially for Micah as he plans for Bar-mitzvah. Also, tell Aunt Elisheva that next year, we all plan to come for Tabernacles, we are just waiting for Liv to get a bit older. And don't forget to tell Aunt Elisheva that we love her and miss her terribly."**

What a good wife, giving last minute reminders to her husband. As if a husband could ever forget those most important details when he goes on a journey. This is what she is talking about.

"Then the angel showed me the river of the water of life, as clear as crystal, flowing from the throne of God and of the Lamb down the middle of the great street of the city. On each side of the river stood the tree of life, bearing twelve crops of fruit, yielding its fruit every month. And the leaves of the tree are for the healing of the nations." Rev. 22:1-2

The following verse from Ezekiel gives us a similar prophetic picture of Jerusalem during the millennium.

"Fruit trees of all kinds will grow on both banks of the river. Their leaves will not wither, nor will their fruit fail. Every month they will bear fruit, because the water from the sanctuary flows to them. Their fruit will serve for food and their leaves for healing." Ezek. 47:12

Frustration Mounting

The Bible teaches that over time even this amazing paradise will be taken for granted. Many mortals will not be thankful for what they have and they will become frustrated because they are not immortal like those who were Christ's at His coming. They will feel like second-class citizens.

They cannot rebel openly against the Lord, because He rules with an iron scepter, but according to God's master plan, the devil will be released to tempt them. He will give them opportunity to follow Satan in rebellion. It will happen just as it happened in the first Garden of Eden. I imagine that Satan will say, **"Do as I tell you, and you will be like God. Together, we will overthrow the Christ and His immortals. We will take over this planet."**

Multitudes will follow Satan's coup to march with him against Jerusalem. Before they even arrive, God will strike them down with fire from heaven.

"When the thousand years are over, Satan will be released from his prison and will go out to deceive

the nations in the four corners of the earth - God and Magog - and to gather them for battle. In number they are like the sand on the seashore. They marched across the breadth of the earth and surrounded the camp of God's people, the city he loves. But fire came down from heaven and devoured them." Rev. 20:8-9

Immediately after the devil is struck down, he will be cast into the lake of fire, and his followers will stand before the great white throne for judgment. Ultimately, they will also be thrown into the fires of hell (see Rev. 20).

The Great White Throne

Following the final battle, at the end of the millennium, all mortals will stand before the great white throne of God Almighty. Those who rebelled against Christ, and remained unrepentant, will be cast into the eternal lake of fire. Those who believed on the Lord Jesus and remained loyal to Him will be given immortality along with those who were Christ's at His coming. I believe they will receive incorruptible bodies at that time (see 1 Cor. 15:23-24).

CHAPTER FIFTEEN

The New Physics

No More Death

When the new millennium is completed and judgment day is finalized, Jesus will hand His kingdom over to God the Father. Little is known of eternity beyond that point. We can speak of the resurrection of the dead and eternal life, but what does that mean moving forward? Let us connect the dots and look into the future as best we can.

From what we know, the science of everything will have to change because there will be no more death. This being said, we should note that angels and God, and even Adam and Eve, for a season, lived without corruption in a universe where death existed. This present universe, the resurrection and eternal life are part of God's plan. Here are a few of the Bible verses that speak of the resurrection, and the end of death itself.

"There will be no more death or mourning or crying or pain, for the old order of things has passed away." Rev. 21:4

"But if there is no resurrection of the dead, not even Christ has been raised." 1 Cor. 15:13

"[After the resurrection] ...He appeared to more than five hundred of the brothers and sisters at the same time..." 1 Cor. 15:6

"The last enemy to be destroyed is death." 1 Cor. 15:26.

"For as in Adam all die, so in Christ, all will be made alive" 1 Cor. 15:22

The most stunning revelation of Scripture is the resurrection of the dead and the immortality that follows. It is not logical because it does not fit the physics or the science of our world.

If a human body has not yet decomposed, we know that modern science may sometimes be able to revive and resuscitate that body with oxygen, electric shock treatment, or some other mechanical application.

That kind of resurrection is not what we are talking about. The Bible speaks of those who have been dead for hundreds of years coming to life again. It even speaks of those whose bodies have disintegrated and been dispersed into billions of particles and spread throughout the sea.

"The sea gave up the dead that were in it, and death and Hades gave up the dead that were in them, and each person was judged according to what they had done." Rev. 20:13

A Gross Illustration

If we seriously think about the resurrection, it becomes an absurd proposal to a logical mind that does not have faith. Please forgive me for giving you the following gross illustration. I suggest that you skip the next couple of paragraphs if you have a weak stomach.

You are still reading! Great! Well, think about a decomposed human body eaten by a fish, and that fish is eaten by another fish. What if that fish is caught by a fisherman and served on someone's dinner plate?

Can you imagine where the mixed up molecules of a human body might end up? It may be recycled in dozens of other animals or people over hundreds of years. Some parts might start off in the Caribbean and end up in Korea. What happens on resurrection day when one person's molecules have now become part of someone else's body? Whose body will they belong to in the resurrection?

Sorry for giving you that uncivilized illustration, but I am trying to make a point about the amazing, miraculous nature of the resurrection.

A Different Body

The Bible gives some details that help bring understanding to this dilemma of the same molecules belonging to different bodies over hundreds of years. Here are some verses. They do not answer all of the questions, but I think they point us in the right direction.

"So will it be with the resurrection of the dead. The body that is sown is perishable, it is raised imperishable; it is sown in dishonor, it is raised in glory; it is sown in weakness, it is raised in power; it is sown a natural body, it is raised a spiritual body." 1 Cor. 15:42-44

According to God's master plan, in the resurrection, we are raised with a spiritual body. Our body is different from what it was in this life. In fact, flesh and blood, as we know it, is not raised to life.

"Flesh and blood cannot inherit the kingdom of God, nor does the perishable inherit the imperishable... we will be changed." 1 Cor. 15: 50,52

"Just as we have borne the image of the earthly man, so shall we bear the image of the heavenly man." 1 Cor. 15:49

"The first man was of the dust of the earth; the second man is of heaven." 1 Cor. 15:47

"It is sown a natural body, it is raised a spiritual body." 1 Cor. 15:44

> *"God gives it a body as he has determined, and to each kind of seed he gives its own body. Not all flesh is the same: People have one kind of flesh, animals have another, birds another and fish another. There are also heavenly bodies and there are earthly bodies; but the splendor of the heavenly bodies is one kind, and the splendor of the earthly bodies is another. The sun has one kind of splendor, the moon another and the stars another; and star differs from star in splendor. So it will be with the resurrection of the dead. The body that is sown is perishable, it is raised imperishable... if there is a natural body, there is a spiritual body."* 1 Cor. 15:38-42,44

The Spiritual Body

After reading Paul's explanation in the verses above, we may conclude that we do not know the kind of resurrected body he is talking about. He explains that God made the bodies of everything we see, some are biological, and some are mineral, but God made them all. Is it therefore possible that there is another kind of body with which we are not familiar? The Bible calls it a spiritual body, a heavenly body.

Concerning this, we are not left in the dark, because Jesus met with His disciples with that kind of resurrected body. We are also told that we will be like Him when He returns.

"When Christ appears, we shall be like him, for we shall see him as he is." 1 Jn. 3:2

I shared some of this next section earlier in the book, but I include it again as a reminder. The Bible says we will be like Him, so here are some of the specifics that are in store for us.

1. We will be immortal (no longer dying) - 1 Cor. 15:53
2. We will be incorruptible (no longer decaying) - 1 Cor. 15:53
3. We will know fully, even as we are known - 1 Cor. 13:12
4. We will have a perfect spirit - Heb. 12:23
5. We will have a new supernatural body, like Christ's - Phil. 3:21
6. Jesus can fly - I imagine we will fly as well - Acts 1:9
7. Jesus was translated from place to place - I imagine we will also - Mt. 28:16-17
9. Jesus walked through walls - I imagine we will also - Jn. 20:26
10. We will be able to travel the cosmos, between planets - Rev. 19:14

These dynamics give us a picture of some of the things a spiritual body can do.

The Resurrection

The resurrection is when our spirits are reunited with our bodies. The body we end up with, however, will be different from the one we had before the resurrection. Everything about us will be upgraded and perfected according to God's plan. The Bible calls it the redemption of the body, and the completion of our sonship.

"We ourselves, who have the firstfruits of the Spirit, groan inwardly as we wait eagerly for our adoption to sonship, the redemption of our bodies." Rom. 8:23

Besides the fact that we will have a spiritual body, other supernatural changes will happen in the universe around us.

No Sun, Moon, or Night

There will be many surprises in the world to come. The Bible says there is no need for the sun, moon, or night. The Lord will be our light and energy source. Here it is, at the end of the Bible, in Revelation chapter twenty-one:

"The city does not need the sun or the moon to shine on it, for the glory of God gives it light, and the Lamb is its lamp... there will be no night there." Rev. 21:23,25

We read of this in the last chapter of Revelation as well.

"There will be no more night. They will not need the light of a lamp or the light of the sun, for the Lord God will give them light." Rev. 22:5

We can only imagine what changes God will have to bring to the science of the universe in order to make these things possible. Dr. Hugh Ross, PHd, of <u>Reasons to Believe,</u> tells us the following:

"The new creation will be bathed in light, but not electromagnetic light. No Sun, Moon or stars will exist (see Isa. 34:4; Rev. 21:22; 22:5). There will be no need for lamps or any other familiar source of illumination (see Rev. 22:5). Nowhere within the new creation will there be any darkness, night or shadows (see Rev. 21:23-22:5). Whereas darkness dominates the present creation, light will permeate the new. Whereas the majority of matter in the present creation absorbs and/or reflects light, everything in the new creation will radiate light.

In the present creation, all the physical laws are linked to thermodynamics, gravity and electromagnetism. So the elimination of all three from the new creation implies the removal of all the physics that govern the universe. Totally new laws will take effect.

When God says, "I am making everything new," he apparently means all the physics and features of the new realm will be radically different from those we are familiar with. The end of sin and evil means physics will no longer need to set boundaries or limit self-expression in work, creativity, play or relationships." (Why The Universe Is The Way It Is, Dr. Hugh Ross Phd, Baker Books, pgs. 197,198, 2001 - used by permission)

God will change the physics of the universe and see to it that there will be no more death.

Everything Dies

In our present universe everything dies; death produces heat, and that heat is needed to produce and sustain life. Stars are dying; they are burning up their fuel. Animals and vegetation die, and the decomposition produces heat. Death brings heat, light, and life, but if there is no more death, then God must find another way to create and sustain life.

God who made it all in the first place, can make it all again, and He can make it different if He wants to. He can recreate everything and put new laws in place. He says that light and life will continue, but those things will come directly from Him and His Son.

Expect a new, different, and better universe. That is God's plan. He will change the laws of physics.

CHAPTER SIXTEEN

World Without End

Out of This World

We cannot hope to explain the distant future of the universe, or our life in the far reaches of eternity, but we can still imagine. The details of God's plans for eternity have not been revealed, but here are a few scriptures that give us some guidelines for dreaming.

"He will be great and will be called the Son of the Most High. The Lord God will give him the throne of his father David, and <u>he will reign over Jacob's descendants forever; his kingdom will never end</u>." Lk. 1:32-33 (Emphasis added)

> *"To Him be glory in the church and in <u>Jesus Christ throughout all ages, world without end</u>." Eph. 3:21 KJV* (Emphasis added)
>
> *"There will be <u>no end to the increase of His government</u> or of peace... from then on and <u>forevermore</u>. The zeal of the Lord of Hosts will accomplish this." Isa. 9:7 NAS* (Emphasis added)

A kingdom is not just a place; it is a king, a multitude of people who serve that king, and the principles of governance over the realm. According to God's plan, Scripture tells us that Christ's kingdom will never end; rather it will be continually growing.

The World is Not Enough

These verses lead us to make some conclusions about the increase that is coming. Earth has a limited amount of space, but God's kingdom will be always expanding. That tells us that, at some point, we must function beyond this planet.

When the Bible was written, humans did not think of venturing to the moon or other planets, but in my lifetime we have landed on the moon and sent probes to the farthest reaches of our solar system. Already, we are planning manned spacecraft missions to Mars. Scientists are designing and working out the logistics for colonies of humans on other celestial spheres. Even though our plans are primitive, it is not farfetched to think that God's plans will have us on other planets and even other solar systems.

Technology and Space Travel

Man used to dream of intercontinental travel and communication; now we experience interplanetary communication and travel.

All of us know that one day the Lord will descend from heaven. That means heaven is up there, somewhere. Satan was cast down from there and angels travel to and fro, from heaven to earth on a regular basis in minutes, hours, or days (see Dan. 10:13). Space travel for spiritual beings does not take weeks, months, or years.

Things that once were part of science fiction continue to push our imagination to new realms of possibility and reality. We have seen hi-tech applications in farfetched movies, but some of them have actually been invented and are now part of our daily lives.

In the 1960's we saw fictional flip-out telecommunicators that allowed someone on a planet to talk to someone on a spaceship. Now, we have cell phones that do much more than that.

We have Facetime on our cell phones so we can see people on the other side of the world while we speak to them and we have hologram technology so it can happen in 3-D. A further surprise to me is that it happens in real time, as if the person we are talking with, on the other side of the world, is present in the room with us.

Through satellite technology we can see and hear just about everything that is happening on the planet. We can read a newspaper in someone's hand from outer space. We can hear a faint whisper spoken inside a house and see a heat image of a person on the other side of a wall. It doesn't matter if it is daytime or nighttime; everything is now visible. There is no longer any privacy in the world. What will it be like in the future? The knowledge of the Lord will cover the earth as the waters cover the sea. What knowledge does He have?

Space Travel

Teleporting of inanimate objects and life forms are fiction now, but who knows what the future holds? Jesus walked through walls or at least appeared on the other side of them without entering through a doorway (see Jn. 20:19). Was that teleporting? Philip instantly found himself in another place many miles away from where he began. It appears that he was teleported (see Acts 8:39).

In the movies we see such imaginary things as portals and wormholes that allow interplanetary travel. In the Bible, we read of gates of heaven and gates of hell. Are there really such things, or is there some interplanetary connection that function like them in the spirit world?

What about space travel with the help of other spirit beings? When Jesus returns to earth, He will be riding a white horse, and all of the armies of heaven will be riding white horses as well (see Rev. 19:14).

I have often wondered why Jesus or angels use these spirit horses to come down from heaven. Do they need them? Is Jesus on a white spirit horse so that He can be with the others who need to be on these white horses to travel through space?

Zechariah tells us that these spirit beings, that look like horses, stand in the presence of God, and that He sends them forth into the world to do His bidding (see Zech. 6:5). Get ready, I think, that in eternity, we will all ride spirit horses; white, red, black or grey ones.

Creators Don't Stop

We are made in God's image, and that is why everyone is an artist and a creator. People do different things; some paint, others compose music, dance, build houses, cook, grow things, write, teach, or invent contraptions. There is no limit to the creative genius that God has put in the human race.

God is the creator and His amazing creativity is unstoppable. Human artists have a compulsion to design, express, and celebrate what they envision. They must create art because they are made in God's image, so it stands to reason that He loves to create art even more than we do.

Can you imagine the Living God being idle, so that He stops creating? I am an artist, with a small letter 'a', but ask my family if I ever stop creating. I cannot. To me, it makes no sense that God would ever stop creating; therefore, I must assume that He will continue to create on a grand scale.

I imagine that He has other inhabitable planets right now and He is creating other spiritual beings constantly. We have only been told what we need to know, but one day we will know much more (see 1 Cor. 13:12).

Ruling and Sharing Government

Scripture promises that if we suffer with Christ, we shall also reign with Him. It tells us that if we have been faithful in little, He will make us rulers over much. Jesus told His followers that the faithful will rule over cities and nations.

What about ruling over planets, solar systems, or even quadrants of galaxies? Even though the universe that is to come will have peace and unity, it will not be run by robots or androids. Learning, training, and rewarding those who excel, will always be part of God's universe, and that requires leadership, mentoring, and management. Who will God give you to train and equip in the worlds to come?

Artists Abound

Manage we will, but God did not make the human race only to manage things, or else we would not have been made in His image. We have been created to create. Mankind has been creating since before the invention of the wheel. Creativity is in our DNA.

What kind of creativity will we experience in the realms of eternity that are before us? Will the Lord allow us to make worlds and solar systems? Even now, I would not be surprised at that amazing possibility. We are not just managers; we are creators!

Art is the creative celebration of some aspect or detail of life. In our world, some artists celebrate evil, but it is still art. One day, evil will be eradicated and then all art will glorify God. Art will be much more amazing in the future; it will be supernatural. Can you imagine; can you dream of supernatural art?

God's New Realm

I can imagine what God will say to His family at that time. He will say what He said to Adam and Eve in the garden, "Be fruitful and multiply." But then, unlike in the garden, our abilities and our fruitfulness will be far beyond our present limitations.

In eternity we will enter God's new realm. It will be the realm of the five graces. As I see it, they are: fellowship, faithfulness, fullness, fabricating, and fruitfulness. When everyone is functioning under God's completed design, we will truly see a world without end.

You will fully adopt God's plan so that His plan will become your plan. Furthermore, your personal plan will become a small part of God's great plan. It is not that He will give you the details of everything you are to do, but rather, He will train you, equip you, and release you.

You have been called to be the fullness of Him who fills all in all. All of us, who are in Christ, are His sons and daughters. We are the extension of His life. He will take great delight in this, for what can be more precious than a family stepping out together in love and unity?

God's Great Plan

"Now unto the King eternal, immortal, invisible, the only wise God, be honor and glory forever and ever. Amen." 1Tim. 1:17

God deserves our highest praise. He is the eternal King; the only wise God. He is immortal and invisible, yet He has revealed His invisible plan, His word, His heart, and His ways to us. His methods, which were far beyond us, have been brought close, so that we can clearly see what He is up to. He has shown us His past, present, and future designs. All of His plans are beyond amazing and once we see them, we can only worship Him with everything we have.

All honor and glory belongs to our God and unto the Lamb, for He has done all things well. Now, and in the unforeseeable future, we have dreams without end, creativity without end, fulfillment without end, fellowship without end, and indeed, a world - no, a universe - without end. So be it - Amen and amen!

Other Titles by Dr. Peter Wyns

Israel's Coming Revival

Unexpected Fire: A Powerful new study on the Book of Revelation

America in the Last Days: The Jonah Nation

Blessings or Curses for the Next Generation

The Powerful Little No Rapture Book: What the Bible says about a Rapture

Poetic Fire: Understanding the Book of Revelation (put to Poetry)

Great Reward for Kids #1: Spiritual Studies for Children

Great Reward for Kids #2: Spiritual Studies for Children

Great Reward for Kids #3: Spiritual Studies for Children

Prayer that Hits the Target

Proclamations for Life: Changing Your Life by Declaring God's Word

Chronicles of Righteousness Volume One: Fifty Powerful Sermons to Help Equip God's People

Chronicles of Righteousness Volume Two: Fifty Powerful Sermons to Help Equip God's People

Chronicles of Righteousness Volume Three: Fifty Powerful Sermons to Help Equip God's People

Fighting Death and Other Desperate Battles

To order, visit www.peterwyns.com or call 803-324-0739.

www.ingramcontent.com/pod-product-compliance
Lightning Source LLC
Chambersburg PA
CBHW070428010526
44118CB00014B/1943